LETTERS TO OLIVE:

SEA OF LOVE, SEA OF LOSS

SEED OF LOVE, SEED OF LIFE

John Quinn was born in Co. Meath. He began his career as a teacher, but later became a radio producer and broadcaster with RTÉ. He has won many prestigious awards for his radio work. John is also an accomplished author of fiction and non-fiction, including children's books. His most recent publication is *The Curious Mind* – a collection of some of his most entertaining and provoking radio interviews and programmes. His childhood memoir, *Goodnight Ballivor, I'll Sleep in Trim*, has also been the subject of a TG4 television documentary.

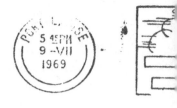

JOHN QUINN
LETTERS
TO OLIVE

*Sea of Love, Sea of Loss
Seed of Love, Seed of Life*

VERITAS

Published 2011 by
Veritas Publications
7–8 Lower Abbey Street
Dublin 1
Ireland

publications@veritas.ie
www.veritas.ie

ISBN 978-1-84730-261-8

Sea of Love, Sea of Loss: Letters to Olive was first published in
2003 by TownHouse, Dublin.

10 9 8 7 6 5 4 3 2 1

A catalogue record for this book is available from the British
Library.

Designed by Barbara Croatto, Veritas
Printed in Ireland by Hudson Killeen, Dublin

*Veritas books are printed on paper made from the wood pulp of
managed forests. For every tree felled, at least one tree is planted,
thereby renewing natural resources.*

Preface

I am delighted that Veritas have agreed to re-issue *Sea of Love, Sea of Loss*, which has been out of print for some years now. This, together with the new volume *Seed of Love, Seed of Life*, will, I hope, give a comprehensive insight into the nature of loss and my own ten-year journey in coping with that loss.

John Quinn

February 2011

Contents

II. SEED OF LOVE, SEED OF LIFE

Foreword

We do not live life without encountering love and loss. Powerful emotions, they define what it is to be human. Love and loss are inextricably connected and recursively bound. As we love so we grieve; the depth of one determining the intensity of the other. One cannot grieve if one cannot love. To live is to love, to love is to live, to lose is to grieve. Love is togetherness. Grief is encountered alone.

In *Letters to Olive: Sea of Love, Sea of Loss; Seed of Love, Seed of Life,* John Quinn invites us to accompany him on an emotional excavation of the twin experiences of love and loss in his own life. It is a journey through grief that is deep because of the depth of love that preceded it. It is a story without an end because when John Quinn fell in love with Olive Rosemary McKeever it was for ever. It was a love for life and beyond. The progress of that love – its serendipitous beginnings, its romantic progression, its everyday challenges, its ordinary expression, its extraordinary depth, its alterations, its difficulties, its faithfulness, fidelity and dramatic, untimely end – is portrayed in this most beautiful narrative.

Letters to Olive includes us in their courtship; the proposal – 'never was a question so obvious [nor] an answer so immediate'; the marriage – 'one day it will delight us to remember these things'; parenthood – 'so proud, so privileged to have you as my wife and mother of our child'; and all the love and life that John and Olive lived together for thirty-three years until Olive's death a decade ago. This book includes us in the spiritual continuation of their relationship to the present day and in John's articulation

9

of grief which is psychologically invaluable, not just for himself, but for everyone who reads this story who has ever groped for meaning in the labyrinths of loss.

At a time in Irish society when courtship sounds quaint, when fidelity is undermined, when love is commodified, when family is often unsupported and marriage vows can be dismantled, *Letters to Olive* is a timely tribute to married love in all its realities. It is also a beautiful testimony to the sustaining presence of those we love – a presence not even death can sever. *Letters to Olive* is a love story made magnificent by its simplicity. It is a life story that is captivating. It is a tribute to the beauty of Olive herself, as person, as wife, as mother, as carer, as life well-lived and courageously so, and as John Quinn's 'one and only love'. It is a tribute to John as a man who has the courage to express publicly his innermost and most intimate experience of loneliness for his wife.

But *Letters to Olive* does not idealise marriage. It also recounts the stresses and strains, the times when love can be dormant – 'are there any fences left to mend?' – and how married love revives when it is given a chance. In so doing, the book invites appreciation of the solid foundation of marriage, the importance of staying with it when times are good and bad, during sickness and health, in tragedy and triumph, just as John and Olive did, articulating for a generation that may need it the wonderful commitment embodied in the words 'I do' and 'until death do us part'.

Grief is a special journey and *Letters to Olive* is a transformative observation of grief. It highlights the commonality as well as the individuality of grief, how each grief, as each life, is unique, regardless of similarities. John Quinn exposes the heart and soul of grief at its most raw and real. He shows how terrifying grief is when, in the words of Emily Dickinson, 'everything that ticked has stopped'. He shows how visceral it is; in physical pain – 'it's beautiful but it hurts'; in the searing of remembrance in a piece of music – 'it links us in a special way'; in lyrics – 'no more talk of darkness, forget those wide-eyed fears'; in a photograph – 'to tell my troubles to'; in sleeplessness, in loneliness, in despair – 'I would prefer to leave and be with you'; and in the anguish of reaching out towards someone no longer visible, but who is also present – 'feel you, hear you, sense you' – in memory.

John's journey through grief exposes our fundamental human vulnerability, our essential frailty, our exceptional strength and the extraordinary capacity to go on by those who, as Amelia Burr wrote, 'have longed for death in the darkness' but who continue for the sake of others and of life itself.

'There is a land of the living and a land of the dead and the bridge is love,' wrote Thornton Wilder, and if anything captures John's Quinn's new and extended edition of *Letters to Olive* it is this. Not since C. S. Lewis's *A Grief Observed*, one of the finest meditations on mourning the death of a wife, has a personal journey through grief been so realistically, courageously, lightly and poignantly written. John's book shows how blessed are those who mourn, lament's fine moments, guilt's descent into hell, the distress of regret, the comfort of memory, dialogue with the departed, pleading with God and the deafening silence with which loneliness replies, before answers and meaning and healing are revealed. Because ultimately this is a book about hope.

If, as poet Philip Larkin once said, 'what will survive of us is love', then John Quinn's *Letters to Olive* ensures that their love that survived a lifetime lives for eternity.

Marie Murray

I. SEA OF LOVE, SEA OF LOSS

For you, Eddie Duchins, who else?
Love you, miss you – above all, thank you.

And it was lovely then
And you were lovely then
And we were young
And so in love
And it was lovely then

Prologue

5 a.m.,
Friday, 29th June 2001

Dawn has broken over Bray. I cannot sleep, so I will write. Dawn has also stolen in from the Irish Sea and crept over Shanganagh Cemetery, just outside Bray, over a new flower-laden grave. My dozen red roses lie on the resting place of my darling Olive Rosemary McKeever, my wife of thirty-three years. It is the end of the most unimaginably traumatic week of my life – unreal, surreal, unbelievable; my beautiful one left me just eighty-four hours ago, at 5 p.m. on Monday, 25th June.

It was Christmas postponed. Just before Christmas 2000, Olive had a horrific fall down a stone stairs, broke her neck, and lost her swallow in the trauma. She was hospitalised for three months, incarcerated in a monstrous metal head-frame – euphemistically called a halo. Given that there was no guarantee that she would ever recover her swallow, Olive was, understandably, suicidal that Christmas. 'This is not Christmas', I told her. 'Christmas will be when you are better.' And she did get better. Ever a fighter, she recovered her swallow and finally shed the halo. But, four days after Olive came out of hospital, her sister Derry died unexpectedly. After all the heartache, Olive deserved a mid-summer Christmas. I booked us into the Great Southern Hotel in Rosslare for two nights, and then into Kelly's on the Strand for six nights. Rosslare has always had a special place in our hearts. When the children were small, we rented a holiday home there for the month of July for successive years. To be going back now and staying in Kelly's … Olive was so excited. I must not tell anyone where we were going … it was to be our secret.

After a very pleasant stay in the Great Southern, we moved into Kelly's on the Sunday afternoon with a mountain of luggage. *[Will I ever forget the number of outfits you brought?]* We checked into our room at 4 p.m. – just in time to watch Meath's resounding victory over Kildare in the Leinster Senior Football Championship.

Olive couldn't bear to watch the game, as usual, but rejoiced in the win, and was so happy when she rang our son, Declan, that evening. We went for a walk on the beach before our first dinner in Kelly's – for which, of course, Olive dressed in head-turning elegance. A Guinness and a port in the bar, and then to bed. For once, Olive slept well, and next morning enjoyed breakfast in bed while I savoured the Monday papers.

It was a warm, humid day. This would be the Alternative Christmas Day. There would be champagne for dinner tonight … We relaxed in the hotel garden. You sipped Tio Pepe while I read from Ben Kiely's *Collected Stories*. Lunchtime. You chided me for going for the full lunch, while you had a bowl of soup and a glass of Guinness. It was leek and potato soup, as I remember. It was a happy lunch. I asked you were you glad you came … we were just getting into the swing of things. It was Christmas Day.

Back to the garden. We move to the shelter of the teahouse. Sound of the surf as we relaxed again. I read Ben Kiely's story, 'A Cow in the House.' You're determined to have that first swim – and in the sea, not in the pool. You send me down to the pool for a towel. *[I sneak an afternoon tea while I'm there!]* You put on your swimsuit and a bathing-cap. I should really go with you, but I have no togs with me. I help you over the rope. You lean on me as I guide you down the dune. *[It is the last time I will hold your living hand.]* You say, 'I'll probably be back in a minute if the water is too cold.' I go back up and watch closely as you wade gingerly into the sea. I can imagine your 'ooohs' as you hit water … you find a depth and go down. I can see your arms do the breast-stroke. Once, twice, thrice, maybe. Then nothing. Your head stays face down in the water. Something is wrong. Jesus – no! Please. No. I race down, call out your name. No response. I race in, drag you out, limp, unconscious. I will always remember how light you felt …

Before I reach the water's edge, others have arrived. Two doctors, a nurse, a lifeguard. They take over. I clutch your bathing-cap, look on, helpless, disbelieving. Please, please don't go. Please let it not be true. Please. They work furiously, thumping your chest. A part of me wants to protest that they are hurting you. There is froth on your mouth. You can't be dead, but I know you are. I can do nothing. I should be talking to you but I freeze. You lie there, limp, bedraggled, lifeless.

The ambulance men arrive. They try to resuscitate you, but it's hopeless. I can't believe it. Won't believe it. People are kind and supportive, especially Billy Kelly and Brenda Sweeney. But you're gone from me – and you never said goodbye … You are taken to the hospital. I go with you on that nightmare journey to Wexford Hospital. What's wrong with me? I can't talk to you. I sit there and stare at you. Numb. All I can do is repeat the mantra – 'Sacred Heart of Jesus, I place her in your eternal loving care'. We reach the hospital. The casualty staff go through the motions of trying to resuscitate you. Futile. I sit by your side, stroking your arm, your mussed hair. The hospital chaplain gives you the Last Blessing. Everyone is so kind. Mary the nurse. Bill Kelly. Brenda and Noel Sweeney, who followed the ambulance. Then the phone calls begin. My brother Noel. Your brother Peter. It isn't happening. But it *has* happened. Eventually I leave. I kiss your lips and withdraw, reluctantly. Numb.

The curate from Rosslare arrives and sits with me. Then the phone calls I dread making to the children. Kelly's staff are wonderful, especially Eddie Cullen, the manager. Noel arrives from Dublin. Approaching midnight, we must make that awful journey back to the hospital to identify you formally to the Gardaí and to make a statement.

To the mortuary chapel. You are wheeled out – still as you were, wrapped in a sheet, your lovely hair still mussed. This is not the way it was meant to be. Unreal, unreal, unreal. We return to the hotel. The heavens echo to a prolonged thunderstorm and the rain comes down in torrents …

CALM

Of course I'm calm –
On the surface.
Only a gentle ripple
Disturbs the quiet waters
Of my life.
But underneath
Deep deep down
There is turmoil.
Shadow beasts
Scythe through the gloom
Unspeakable monsters
Lurk in cavernous lairs
Among bottomless, bottomless
Depths.
So take my hand
And tread water with me
Teach me to be calm
Like when you taught
Our children to swim.
Assuage my fears
Help me to be calm
But not
Becalmed.

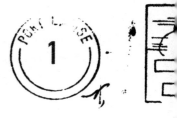

1

The Beginning of the Adventure

Of course, dear reader, you remember where you were on 22nd November 1963, when an assassin's bullets echoed around the world? But can you remember where you were exactly two years later – 22nd November 1965? I can, because it was a defining day in my life.

I presented myself for admission to James Connolly Memorial Hospital, Blanchardstown, Dublin – affectionately known to its inmates as the Blanch – a sanatorium for the treatment of tuberculosis. TB had ravaged the country in the 1930s, 40s and 50s, before its advance was checked by developments in medicine and the building of a number of sanatoria like the Blanch. In his book, *Ireland Since the Rising*, Tim Pat Coogan notes how the slum-dwellers of Dublin gave much of the credit for this to Dr Noel Browne, TD – 'the man that gave us the free TB'.

I was a few weeks short of my twenty-fourth birthday, a primary teacher, earnest and diligent in my work and study (three weeks earlier, I had been conferred with a BA degree, pursued through evening classes), but also gauche and not very wise in the ways of the world.

In the summer of 1965, I had been on a five-week study-tour in the United States with a group of teachers. It had been a marvellous experience – three weeks' residency in New York State University and two weeks on tour – Niagara, Chicago, Philadelphia and Washington. We were guests in the White House and the Capitol, meeting President Johnson, Bobby and Ted Kennedy, former President Eisenhower and many others – a once-in-a-lifetime experience that certainly helped me develop

socially. I remember, on the flight home, trying to arrange a date with one of the women teachers, who told me I was very talented, but that I didn't give of my talents enough and that I needed to be much more outgoing. I told her that, 'at home', I was very shy and had an inferiority complex. She refused to believe this. She also refused me the date (the 'line was engaged'), which, of course, further punctured my self-esteem.

Come September, I resumed teaching and – true to form – began studying at night in UCD for a Higher Diploma in Education. Teaching and study – and very little social life. I developed a persistent cough that caused some annoyance, but little bother otherwise. So, when the mobile X-ray unit visited Earlsfort Terrace one November evening (an indication of how real the TB threat still was), more for fun than anything else, I joined a few friends to 'have our photographs taken'. The fun quickly dissolved a week or two later when I was summoned for a second X-ray. A shadow had been detected on one lung and, even though I had no symptoms other than the cough and did not feel ill, the message was clear: I had TB and would have to spend some time in Blanchardstown. How much time was not clear. Three months? Six months? Nine? A year? It was all very uncertain and not a little unreal. It was a particularly hard blow for my mother as, a few weeks earlier, my father had been taken to hospital with a heart attack.

So, it was a somewhat bemused and nervous young man who was admitted to Ward 5, Unit 2, on that November evening, to join Dan, Jimmy, Ned, Arthur and Paddy – just in time for 'rest hour', from 5–6 p.m., followed by a 'boiled egg tea'. It was a Monday evening, so the three young men who were 'on grade' were allowed go to the weekly film show after tea. It gave me the opportunity to discuss life in the Blanch with the older men – Ned and Paddy – and, in good dutiful teacher fashion, to write out notes on my Finglas students for the benefit of my successor.

Dr Monica Clay welcomed me to Blanchardstown. Across the Atlantic Ocean, her namesake, Cassius, would successfully defend his World Heavyweight Boxing crown, while I would – hopefully – sleep.

SOMETIME, ONETIME

Sometime, onetime
When we were young
I wonder did our paths
ever cross?
In Navan maybe
At a football match,
Or in a sweetshop
–Tierney's? –
In Slane
At a McMaster pageant?
Or later –
Did you pass
St Patrick's on a bus
Airport-bound?
And catch a glimpse
Of a shy, awkward student
Who wondered if
Sometime, onetime
He might meet and love
Someone like you?

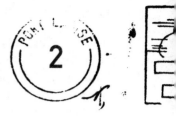

2

Life in 'the Blanch'

Blanchardstown Hospital was built on a similar model to other sanatoria of the 1950s – Merlin Park in Galway and Ardkeen in Waterford. Twelve forty-bed, single-storey units and a three-storey hospital building set in a wooded estate. The units were strictly segregated on a gender basis – apart from the children's unit. Treatment consisted of rest, medication – and fresh air. (It took a while to get used to ward doors onto a veranda being left open, day and night.) The regime was strict. Rest hours were hours of rest, regularly policed by the sister-in-charge. There was a hospital radio service available on headphones, but transistor radios were banned. This led to a constant cat-and-mouse battle between Sister and the younger patients, with regular confiscation of the offending transistors. I was lucky to escape such confiscation, and found the radio a great comfort and companion during my sojourn – little realising that, ten years later, I would launch out on a career in radio.

The rules and restrictions of sanatorium life reminded me of the boarding-school life I had left only six years previously. Of course, the regime was for our good – we were there to be made well. But when romance would later enter the equation, it proved more than frustrating. Dr Holmes, the Medical Officer, was very keen for me to continue my Higher Diploma in Education studies, and made a special appeal to UCD on my behalf. The appeal was turned down, and reading for leisure, rather than for academic ends, became more important for me. That was, of course, when I wasn't involved in exciting occupational therapy pursuits, such as the construction of fruit baskets from lollipop sticks and toy furniture from matchboxes. On a more cerebral level, French and German lessons were available on the hospital radio service but, again, this was leavened by admittedly less challenging, but more pleasurable, pursuits such as 'penny-in' games of cards and (courtesy of an understanding porter) regular wagers with the village bookmaker.

Life was slow-paced and reasonably tolerable in the Blanch. I was slowly initiated into institutional life – salt and holly leaves in my bed (shades of boarding school again). Christmas came and slowly went. It was my first Christmas away from home, and it was a lonely time. And all the time, unknown to me, just a field away in Unit 4 lay someone who would ultimately put an end to my loneliness.

Visitors did help. Even though the sanatorium was quite a distance from the city, family and work colleagues came regularly, often bearing gifts of much-sought home cooking, which relieved the predictable tedium of the hospital menu. Incredibly, the visitors regularly brought cigarettes, for this was the 1960s and most of us were regular smokers. Smoking was allowed, even though many of us were being treated for disease of the lung (including Kevin, whose lungs had been described by Dr Holmes as being like 'lace curtains'). Alcohol was prohibited, but that did not prevent 'fourteen dozen of stout' being consumed in Unit 2 on Christmas Eve. I, being a non-drinker, did not partake and retired to my bed with an illicit transistor. Sister had her revenge on St Stephen's Day, however, when, with all the cunning of a customs officer, she intercepted twenty-six bags of beer.

Visiting hour had its humorous moments, too. I remember an obviously fearful visitor approaching Andy from our ward with a hankie over his mouth, asking where patient so-and-so was. Quick as a flash, Andy whipped out a hankie to cover *his* mouth before giving the required information.

I have always considered my sojourn in Blanchardstown to be a major part of my education. For a raw, callow young fellow to be cast among a collection of the charming and cantankerous, young blades and hardened 'chaws', the wise and the world-weary, and to live in close proximity with them for nine months – it could not be otherwise. I spent evenings listening to old men recall the

Dublin of their youth ('D'yis remember the Fountain Cinema?'), sharing stories and tall tales:

> Jimmy: 'I'm tellin' yis – it was a busload of skeletons!'
> John C: 'Must have been Christmas – they were down to a skeleton staff!'

And enduring John Coates' (a great big loveable burly Dub) permanent restlessness to be out in the world again: 'I've worked out that, while I'm in the Blanch, I'll have consumed 4,032 tablets, a five-gallon drum of Streptomycin and 779 rings of black puddin'.

For some, the restlessness was short-lived. There were regular examples of fellows who 'did a bunk' after one night in the Blanch. They could not face up to nine months' incarceration.

For others, the outside world would never be a reality again. Paddy, in the bed next to me, died four hours after we heard the bells ring in 1966. It was my first experience of death at close hand. It was the first of a succession of deaths I would witness over the next six months.

A sort of life, painful death, laughter, tears, bonhomie, fun, friction, frustration, loneliness; they were all about me, contributing to my development, my education. And if that were not enough, into my life on a raw March afternoon walked a vision in a black leather coat.

3

The Black Leather Coat

Every few weeks, we were sent down by ambulance to the hospital block for a swab test – a rather indelicate exercise in which one had to cough up sputum which would then be tested 'positive' or (hopefully) 'negative'. Indelicacy apart, we looked on the trip as a break in the routine of sanatorium life. I had been for a number of these outings in my first few months in Blanchardstown, but nothing remotely exciting had ever happened. The 1st March 1966 would change all that. My diary records the event thus:

Then came the girls. A smasher from Unit 4 – Miss McKeever. Phhorr! Must investigate! Actually let the door close in her face as I was dashing to hear the commentary on the Leopardstown Chase ... Arkle beat Height of Fashion by a neck.

Not the most romantic circumstances for a first meeting. Not even a meeting. I don't think we even spoke to each other. I had Arkle on my mind, but she *was* a smasher! Stunningly beautiful. Elegant, with the walk of a queen. And she wore a black leather coat. In a drab hospital building where tawdry woollen dressing gowns were the mode, she wore a black leather coat. In this instance, height of fashion won at a canter!

Like many an impressionable young fellow, I had fallen in and out of love with a succession of nurses during my first three months in the sanatorium. This was different. The vision in the black leather coat totally bowled me over. Miss McKeever. The only people with that surname that I was aware of were Fr McKeever, the parish priest of Trim, Co. Meath, and Peter McKeever, the former Meath footballer. How thrilled I was to discover that the former was her uncle (who, in the space of the next ten years, would marry us and baptise our three children) and the latter was her brother. A wonderful start. Further investigation elicited that she was Olive, 'a lovely girl in every way … very bright … speaks a number of languages … worked in Aer Lingus and on the Cunard Line'. My elation was tempered somewhat. Out of my depth here, I thought. What interest could a glamorous, much-travelled woman like that have in a gauche, reclusive fellow like me? I was smitten. I would make an effort. But how?

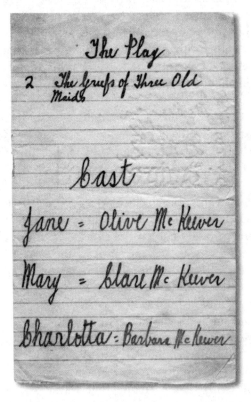

A little treasure from Olive's childhood: a handwritten 'programme' (price 2d) of an entertainment she put on for the family with her twin sisters, Barbara and Clare.

We were both confined to our respective units – except for exotic swab-test outings. I made a start by putting in requests on the Tuesday hospital radio request programme. I soon discovered I had competition for Olive's interest. Any attempts at subtlety or coded messages went over the DJ's head. I was furious with him when he made a total mess of my brilliant (or so I thought) request of 8th March. Nelson's Pillar had been blown up the previous night. I put in a request sending 'Greetings to Charlie Parnell from Dan O'Connell and all your friends down the road. Haven't seen you for ages!' The DJ hadn't a clue what I was on about. No, a more direct approach was needed. I would be bold and write to the fair Olive. I would be even bolder – and hopefully impress the multilingual beauty – by writing in German! In German? Well, it would be a way of putting my meagre language skills to use. Amazingly, I still have the first draft of the '*brief auf Deutsch*' … How I cringe when I read it now.

> *Ich komme aus Co. Meath, genau wie Sie.*
> [I come from Co. Meath, just like you.]

> *Hoffentlich höre ich bald von Ihnen.*
> [Hopefully I will hear from you soon.]

Yeuch! To cover all my options, I hastily wrote a second letter in English. The next problem was the postal system. I had to depend on an understanding nurse or porter to smuggle the letters into Ward 5, Unit 4. (How the echoes of boarding school keep creeping into this story.)

Now came the waiting period. Five days later, the reply came, addressed to 'Herr J. Quinn'. Joy of joys! It was a cautious reply, but I instantly warmed to her style, her ironic touches.

Unit 4,
Blanchardstown,
Saturday, 26th March 1966

Dear John,
Thank you for both your letters. The second one was not requested
(who was casting aspersions on my ability to understand German!)
but welcome. It saved me the effort of having to compose a missive
in Deutsch!
 The grapevine has obviously been hard at work. Full marks for
your detection work to date regarding county of birth, place of
employment, etc. Thank you for your good wishes concerning my
conference next Wednesday. I do hope to get grade. Naturally, the
upsetting news of the long wait to your grade and obviously
interesting company has made the prospect seem not as exciting as
it might be!
 It's nice to know I have brought some brightness into your life.
My term in Blanchardstown will not be in vain after all! Full marks
for the closing line in your letter – don't intend to compete!

Olive

Note 1: I wish I could remember that closing line.
Note 2: 'Getting grade' in Blanchardstown meant that one was
allowed up for walks, trips to the shop, cinema, church, etc. It was
a step nearer the exit gate.

This could be the start of something big. This *was* the start of
something big. For the next three months, the letters would go
back and forth – always addressed to Fraulein Olive and Herr John.
Wonderful letters that, for a start, relieved the tedium of
sanatorium life. Wonderful, wonderful letters where we gradually
unfolded our personalities and learned about each other.
 Olive was put on Grade 4 about a month later. She was ecstatic
about being allowed out for walks. A little taste of freedom. The
walks brought her around by Unit 2 on occasion, which allowed us
the opportunity to exchange a wave or – even more daring – a brief

few words at some distance, she from the road, me leaning from the bathroom window. She would, of course, never be allowed to enter Unit 2. The only way through this frustration was to write longer and more frequent letters. Adding to the frustration were the comments of my fellow inmates as Olive passed by. I did enjoy those of Eugene, who had recently joined us. Eugene and I shared an interest in horse-racing. He would train his (pretend) binoculars on '*Huile d'Olive*' (as he called her) and give a Peter O'Sullevan commentary on how well the Oaks favourite was moving on the gallops this morning. As the weeks slid by and our 'relationship' became known, the teasing increased on all sides. One nurse berated me for the distress I was causing Sr Mary Olive McKeever, Irish Sister of Charity. For a moment, she almost convinced me. But then, no Sister of Charity would sprinkle perfume on her letters to Herr John Quinn and write on the envelope: 'Thought it was time to have you scent again.'

How I loved those little 'postmarks':

'Smile! It has arrived!'

'Bingo! Bingo! Bingo!'

'No postman! Now rain! Life!!'

Paradise Island,
Wednesday, 7 p.m.

Dear John,
Ich bin sehr lustig und – *on second thoughts, bingo to the Deutsch lark! Don't feel I want to be confined by pidgin language today. I feel utterly on top of the world and see everything through a gorgeous haze. Yes, the door has begun to open – OLIVE HAS GOT GRADE!*

Why can't I hear the cheers from Unit 2? Never mind, I'm cheering enough for everyone. Eileen says if I don't stop grinning my face will never be the same again! Don't say it! On two occasions today I have trekked to the bathroom for the express purpose of signalling the news to you. What happened? Nothing – absolutely no response. In disgust I retreated to share my joy with a more receptive audience. Their enthusiasm is now beginning to wear a bit thin – hence my decision to shout my news to you. Aren't you lucky?

Oh, I have just remembered my big grudge and subsequent decision not to write again. How could you (sob!) share my tender passages with other people? (smile breaking through) In my present expansive mood I have decided to forgive you. Stop! Andy is looking over your shoulder – nasty, nasty, nasty!

Yesterday my first big thrill of the day was a letter from you. Then (my hand is shaking with emotion!) I actually saw you pass my window! Phew – it was almost too much – not quite though – why did you not come in?? No, you didn't upset my meditations – only changed their general direction!

My feelings are too effervescent for expression on paper – pity you aren't here! Do you think I'm naughty? I feel wonderful, wonderful, wonderful! Must go, the celebration party is starting …

Yours sincerely,
Sister Mary Olive McKeever!!

How I loved those letters. How I suddenly loved life in the Blanch. How I was growing to love Sr Mary Olive.

Grade 4 could not come quickly enough for me. In the meantime, there was the promise of being allowed out to Mass on Easter Sunday – our first real meeting. My diary records that meeting thus:

Olive a major distraction at Easter Mass – but I tried to concentrate (on Mass!). Afterwards, the big moment! Had to introduce myself to Olive. Pat and I walked 'home' with Olive and Eileen. Far, far too little time. We talked about life in the Blanch, etc., but couldn't get down to important things. Final chat outside Unit 4. Sr Moran was on duty, so no crumpets and tea! *Au revoir.* Verdict – a really lovely girl – looks, manner, personality, the lot – but somehow I felt I was out of my depth! Too good for me? Although neither of us were the people we are in our letters. Again, the time was all too brief, and I must wait four more weeks till grade! However it was a big thrill. It remains to be seen what her letters will be like now! On the radio, 'Bye Bye Blues'. Enough said!

However, Olive's next letter gave me hope.

I am so glad to hear I came up to expectations – I was waiting with bated breath for the verdict! Have just remembered you said 'above expectations' – nicer still! Now what nice things can I say to you so we can form a mutual admiration society! Being honest, I found it slightly disconcerting to be confronted by someone I had been scribbling nonsense to without thought. I was lucky though, my 'unknown' correspondent was you and who could ask for anything more!! Seriously though, brief though our meeting was, I enjoyed it. Happy Easter all over again!

Olive

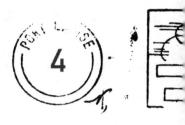

A New Life

There was another unexpected bonus outing on the Thursday after Easter. I was allowed out to attend an Easter 1916 commemoration concert. It was a terrific concert, but the best part was walking Olive 'home', huddled under an umbrella, battling against wind and rain. Oh, it was lovely, until a spoilsport ambulance driver insisted that Olive take a lift and left me walking the streets in the rain, but not before Olive slipped me a letter. I floated home.

Unit 4,
Tuesday, 3rd May 1966

Dear John,
How difficult it is to come down to earth, take up my pen and write in a sober manner. Your latest missive is responsible for my present exalted state – 14 pages! I feel as if all my birthdays have come at once. The 'more, more, more – soon, soon, soon' is re-echoed a thousand times.

Am not sure what shroud you wish me to unveil – will I? won't I? Madly daring, I begin. I was attached to the Purser's Staff of the Queen Elizabeth. Had been at sea almost a year when the blow fell. In that period we did a Caribbean cruise (gorgeous) and an extensive Mediterranean cruise. Prior to joining Cunard I worked as a ground hostess for Aer Lingus, so in one way or another my work has always been connected with travel. My biggest thrill travel-wise was a visit to South Africa. Loved the country and climate and the great highlight was a few days spent in Kruger Park.

My enjoyment was greatly tempered by the awful colour bar – the 'No Blacks Allowed' signs plastered all over the place. Came home and went through a period of reading Late Have I Loved Thee *and* Naught For Your Comfort. *Sorry – Sorry – must not start on that subject – it makes me see red!*

Big Event of Yesterday – John actually braved the inner sanctum of Unit 4! The ensuing excitement – the quickened heartbeats! – but we would still like more. One fly in the ointment – it wasn't Olive he came to see! No – alack and alas – another rival comes into the picture [I was delivering a textbook to a fellow-patient, Colette]. *Can I bear it? – that is the question.*

Mary has just come back from her conference and she goes home on Saturday. Ward 5 has gone mad! Talking of conferences brings to mind yours – between crossing fingers and curling toes (do you ever curl your toes?), daily treks to the church and all my pennies going on candles – well you just have to get grade! Sudden thought – perhaps I'm overdoing it. You might get home and where will poor Olive be then? Never mind, she will be brave and smile for your good fortune …

It's chaos here in Ward 5 so I must end … How about a romantic ending and Omar Khayyám to the rescue!

> Here with a loaf of bread beneath the bough
> A flask of wine, a book of verse – and thou
> Beside me singing in the wilderness –
> And wilderness is paradise enow.

It filled the page! Seven pages – a record for me!

Love, Olive

Those letters consumed my days and nights. I would spend hours writing epistles of ten, twelve, fourteen pages – and loved every minute of it. Suddenly, life had a focus and a purpose! Just to make this wonderful girl happy. I rewrote *Romeo and Juliet* set in a sanatorium, where we were the principal players; the hospital chaplain, Fr Mulligan, became 'the Friar'; and Sr Moran was 'the

Nurse' who thwarted our best efforts on 'the balcony' (hospital veranda). Olive loved it and pleaded for 'more, more, more'. She would regularly conclude her letters with a verse from Omar Khayyám –

> Ah love, could thou and I with fate conspire
> To grasp this sorry scheme of things entire,
> Would not we shatter it to bits – and then
> Remould it nearer to the Heart's desire.

I was growing bolder. I was wondering about life, post Blanchardstown …

You fade away into 'nothingness'?? Impossible – once known, never forgotten! The idea of you fading away into obscurity is too ridiculous to be even considered. How could I possibly forget you? My stay in Blanchardstown has been made so much more pleasant since your entry into my world. What more could I possibly say? Reassured? Good! (What is he saying under his breath?)

What more to say? Your vision at the window this morning – nice! Talk rather limited though – felt very hurt that you refused my invitation to come walking! Terry is much improved since she received a message from you. I think I will have to do something to get thought of 'every minute'!

Your epistles get better and better. More and more and more please – soon, soon, soon!

Love, Olive

We were definitely tuned to the same wavelength, although she was the more sensible one, recognising that we were in a vulnerable position, enclosed in an unreal world. When she wrote, 'you are a special person; pity we didn't meet in another time, another place', she was being realistic, but it depressed me. On reflection, I feel we would *never* have met in another time, another place.

We were an odd couple, really. She was very outgoing, a 'people person', who loved to socialise and was very much travelled. I was shy, somewhat reclusive, dedicated to work and study – a nerd, in modern parlance, I suppose. Yet we resonated off each other so well. Olive certainly opened me out, encouraged my writing talents, took me totally out of myself. Our meeting in the Blanch was meant to be – I am certain of that.

The days, weeks, dragged by. When would I get on Grade 4?

Monday, 9th May – late, late p.m.

Most disappointed – no wave from you on the way home from the pictures. Poor Olive on last legs (how many have I got?) with my sad tale of woe to explain the non-arrival of mail. Reception cool. Sympathy nil. Ned just didn't believe my story (that I had a nasty fall this morning) – and so with great personal risk I sit up and write. Notice tears mixed with ink? Seriously though, I will have to admit I am a total dead loss (got that in before you could!) – falling by the wayside in your time of dire need. Do you think you might have it in your heart to forgive me? You will? Ah – relief, relief! Where was I when the lights went out? With you – how could I forget! Really, I would get first prize for drivel any day …

Someone, somewhere is thinking of you. You are not alone. Everything is going to be alright – it's just got to be. Please, please let me have the news (of your X-ray) as soon as possible – by other means than you suggest!

Love, Olive x

P.S. Like being spoiled – you must do it again!

My wardmate, Andy Penston, brightened life up with his humour and sense of fun. He brightened it further by executing a daring raid on Unit 4 and photographing the glamorous blonde in Ward 5. I now had a portrait to drool over! Life was further brightened by the arrival in Unit 2 of a most attractive and caring night nurse, Ann McGarry, who would subsequently become a lifelong friend of Olive and myself. Ann was a breath of fresh air. Never one to be bound by regulations, she would regularly make soup at midnight for the young blades of Ward 5. It was such a change to be treated as adults. I remember saying at Ann's wedding, years later, that I would forever associate her with celery soup – and I do. Ann also encouraged my romance, claiming that Olive was smitten too and 'madly keen'.

Unit 4,
Sunday

Dear John,

How could you possibly doubt my delight in receiving your missives? When I think of all my efforts (sweat and toil!) in telling you so – and now to hear it was a wasted labour … Words fail me! I give up, retire from the scene of battle, etc., etc.

Coming Events of Note! In two weeks time, John will be on 'grade' and in eight weeks time Olive goes home – all said with fingers and toes crossed! I wonder what effect 'grade' will have on you (am I treading on dangerous ground here?). I know it has made me feel restless. The first six months here have passed in a haze of make-believe, the outside world fading away into nothingness. Now that the end is in sight, I find my thoughts wandering to things beyond the bounds of my confinement. What about you? Has your sojourn here made any difference to you as a person? Goodness, I'm going all serious – apologies – won't let it happen again.

Radio Requests – I am utterly disgusted with them! Each week I spend a lot of my precious time in thinking up some line of wit for you and all to no avail. My genius remains undiscovered – most frustrating! The only ray of sunshine last week was 'Umbrella Man's' request. Message received – over and out. I have decided not to disillusion Mary over your so romantic request of last Tuesday. Thought it would be unfair as I had already made her the recipient of a black eye! Incidentally you will be meeting her on Tuesday – that is, if I don't succeed in keeping her chained!!

What next? Ah yes – your ambiguous comments passed in French. Now, John, don't you realise I am only a simple country girl and cannot be expected to understand all this crosstalk of yours! 'Strings to one's bow,' etc. – whatever is he talking about???

My brief glimpse and short conversation with you this morning has excited me too much to write any more! Must fill the page – what more can I say – nothing – pity – the more dashes the better! Well you played a mean trick on me – sending me an empty envelope on April 1st!!

From 'We're just good friends' – your idea!

Love, Olive

P.S. Olive loves (wait for it – no jumping to conclusions!) receiving letters from John.

What an enthralling letter! She really was a rogue. My diary entry for that day recorded a new hope:

A 'missive' from Olive. As I read the opening lines the radio poured out 'Just Friends' ... ominous. A very clever and funny letter. That girl has got what it takes. It gave me a big charge. From what I gather, all is not lost – yet! Will have to read and re-read it! Thanks Olive – good to know somebody cares. Disrupted all my study plans for the night! Later on the radio – 'I'm in the Mood for Love'. Enough!

Finally, on 11th May 1966, came the long-awaited good news. Dr Holmes put me on Grade 4 and said I could go home in three months. Hallelujah! Freedom to roam the wilds of Blanchardstown! Freedom to meet Olive – at Mass, at the movies, at bingo!

The very first meeting came the following evening, when I sat beside her at bingo. We both agreed that the bingo was a nuisance but, otherwise, it was a wonderful evening. I walked her home, to a chorus of catcalls and slagging from Unit 6. Did I care? Not a whit. Every second in Olive's company was precious and too short. Sunday afforded another opportunity to meet after Mass. My diary entry for that day says it all:

Olive suggested the itinerary – down to the hospital, up by Units 7, 12, 10 – through the woods and 'home' by Unit 6. Wonderful, wonderful – still too short. She's a terrific girl – loved just being with her, talking, laughing. Is it mutual? I hope so. This could well be it – I hope so! Thanks, thanks, thanks. Olive – you're a pet!

And then Monday night was cinema night. Life could hardly get better! The movies were not exactly screen classics:

> Norman Wisdom in *The Bulldog Breed*.
> William Holden in *Father was a Bachelor*.
> Tyrone Power in *The Eddy Duchin Story*.

But what did that matter? It was an opportunity to be together – except when an unknowing older patient insisted on sitting between us. The Tyrone Power film gave rise to a particular term of endearment. 'Poochens' was Olive's term. I converted it (*à la* Cockney slang) to 'Eddie Duchins', as in 'I love you, Eddie Duchins' *[P.S. Still do, more than ever]*. The most wonderful movie night of all, though, was the night there was no movie. Again, my diary tells it best:

Monday, 30th May 1966

Heavenly weather. Lucky for the 'normals' outside who can enjoy it! We knew there would be no film tonight, but no one actually told us that ... So, Pat and I dressed up and hit the road. Olive and Terry from Unit 4 did the same. Being the grand evening it was, we went for a walk – Olive and I leading, Pat and Terry lagging behind. Down to the mortuary – exotic or what! Who passes us in his car but Dr Holmes! Good night! Well, we might as well make a night of it – so, over the gate and through the woods! An absolute panic – over and under fences, through briars, me beating a path, Olive in her high heels. The laughter must have been heard all over the place.

   Several wrong turnings later, we emerged at the Boiler House – the summit of exotica! Olive and I walked round and round the Boiler House lawn – sixteen times, according to Terry – and had a great conversation. It was magic! At eight o'clock we had to part. Pat and I returned to base. Sister was livid. She had been looking everywhere for us. 'In future, don't go to the pictures until I tell you!' Nurse Callaghan warned us that trouble was coming – Sister was reporting us to Dr Holmes (Hee hee! She doesn't have to!)

I couldn't care less. I had a ball. We may have broken the rules – stupid rules – but have no regrets. As Olive said – some day we'll look back and laugh at this. Reminds me of a line from Virgil:

> *Haec olim meminisse iuvabit* – one day it will delight us to remember these things.

It was a defining evening for Olive too.

I'm lost in a maze of mixed-up thoughts and feelings. Firstly (one must begin someplace!) at the start of our correspondence I never for a second thought things could be as they are. How are they? I don't know and hate having to attempt to analyse the whys and wherefores of our friendship. Am afraid something will be lost in the process. For myself, in a gradual way, our meetings and receiving your letters, etc. (we're back to 'etc.' again!) have come to mean quite something to me.

Sorry to hear via Terry you had to endure a lecture on your return from the woods. Feel a bit guilty since it was my suggestion in the first place. I know I would not have missed it for anything. The situation was so ridiculous. I could have curled up with laughter – all right, I did! Thank you for the request. Yes, my head is still spinning – how about yours?

Had the embarrassment of having to face Dr Holmes on my own in the office yesterday morning. He didn't say anything but had a very knowing smile on his face, which put me off completely. Didn't ask him half of what I wanted to ...

Until the next time,
Love, Olive xxx

P.S. Fr Mulligan was told about our venture. He was most amused and came up yesterday to find out if the 'operation' was successful!

Olive had indeed plenty to ask Dr Holmes. A week earlier, the bombshell had dropped. Instead of going home in a few weeks, she was being sent for surgery. Why this happened, I still don't know. All I know is that I felt shattered for Olive. She must have been devastated, but never showed it. She remained in good spirits, and spoke of the upcoming surgery as if it were a visit to the dentist. If anything, the news drew me closer to her. I wrote longer and longer letters. I wanted to comfort her, be a support to her. I was growing increasingly restless and frustrated, especially after the 'taste of living' in our adventure in the woods. I was totally besotted with this beautiful woman who, to me, was 'full of the milk of human kindness'. I couldn't believe my luck – that she should be interested in me! I would do anything for her – despite an edict that came down from Matron, telling of her concern about 'patients mingling'. My reaction at the time was, 'Why don't they send us all to Unit 8 *[the children's unit]*?'

Olive was moved to the hospital in preparation for her operation – which meant our meetings were fewer. I remember a surreal day – Thursday, 9th June. Olive had to undergo a bronchoscopy – I thought of, prayed for and wrote to her all day long. It was the feast of Corpus Christi, and there was to be a procession through the sanatorium grounds, for which purpose loudspeakers had been set up on the procession route. However, it teemed rain all day and the procession was cancelled. Somehow, the loudspeakers were connected to the radio, and we had the wonderfully surreal sound of an Acker Bilk concert echoing all over the grounds through the incessant rain! It caught my own mood perfectly.

Our final 'outing' was the day before Olive's operation. We went for a walk to the Boiler House (now known as Inspiration Point) and had a frank discussion on our respective feelings. Olive was so full of warmth and understanding – we would definitely meet in 'another time, another place'. Fate would intervene first, however.

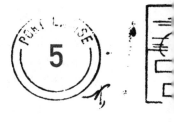

Leaving Blanchardstown

On the day of Olive's operation, I received the news that my father had suffered a stroke and was seriously ill. Following a hastily arranged medical conference, I was allowed home (a month before the allotted time) on compassionate grounds. So, on 24th June, I left Blanchardstown, after a confinement of 215 days. They were very precious days to me. I had discovered myself and I had found the love of my life. Ten days later, my father died. I grieved for him greatly. He was a good, honest, upright man. I was also greatly concerned for Olive. I wanted to be with her, but could not. It later transpired that she almost died when she began to haemorrhage after the operation. I only learned subsequently that she had the entire lung removed – a particularly barbarous operation in those days – but she came through it all in true fighting style, and when I did eventually get to visit her, she looked – as ever – a million dollars.

Even in extreme pain, she managed to write to me.

Hospital 3,
J.C.M.H.,
July 1966

Dear John,
I am terribly sorry to hear your very sad news. Words are inadequate to convey how I feel for you at such a time. It's so much easier to comfort children – you can pick them up, hug them, dry their tears and to a certain extent ease their pain. It's a pity we're not all children at times.

I know you will be able to accept God's will – however hard. You have such a wonderful character. I pray for your father, R.I.P., for you and your family.

Take care of yourself.
God bless.
Love, Olive x

The visits continued over the summer until Olive was eventually discharged in September. She had been in Blanchardstown for a year. In the same week, I resumed teaching. The letters continued too. I wrote almost daily for the next two years. It was October before we had our first date outside Blanchardstown. I drove to Stackallen, full of apprehension at the thought of meeting Olive's parents – needlessly of course. I think her father initially looked on me as one of Olive's 'lost causes'. Her family teased her as being the 'Patron of Lost Causes', such was her concern for the down-and-outs and misfits who crossed her path. She railed against injustice and spoke out against it, often to the embarrassment of her family. I must have been particularly nervous that evening, as Olive's father later told me he considered me a 'one hundred to one shot, who came from nowhere on the rails'. Olive had no shortage of suitors. I was just another one and certainly did not impress her father that October evening. The date itself was a near disaster. We drove to Howth, which was enveloped in a peasouper fog. It wasn't the end, thankfully, but the beginning of a beautiful courtship.

Such was the severity of Olive's operation, she had been advised to spend two years in recuperation. Fate again intervened, as it had in my case. A few months into that recuperation, Olive's mother suffered a stroke and needed constant care. Olive's role changed from being nursed to being a nurse. Her sisters helped out, of course, within their own work patterns, but Olive was often on her own with a very difficult patient. It scarred Olive psychologically, ruining her sleep pattern for the rest of her life. Her sisters Maeve and Joan would take over at weekends, thus freeing Olive to come up to Dublin with me. They were wonderful weekends of togetherness and deepening love. How I hated leaving her back to Stackallen on Sunday evenings!

Harmonstown House,
Stackallen,
Thursday, 9th November 1967

My dearest John,
Thank you so much for your letters (received two of them today) and Mass Bouquet. Words could not express how much they mean to me and how much they have helped me over the last few days. But, without any letters, just the thought of you is enough to keep me going at any time. Darling, I love you so very much and I count the blessings of our mutual love every day. I know I am not expressing my feelings as I would wish but also know you will understand – thank God!

Mother is in a much happier state. She has become very quiet and very weak. Maeve and I take turns at staying with her. Today I managed to get out in the air for a while. It was lovely to walk through the fields and think of you …

Will spoil myself and phone you now! Please don't feel you have to write. I know you are thinking of me and that is the main thing. Re. the weekend – I'm hoping to make Dublin but won't know until Friday. Longing to see you then.

Please take care.
All my love,
Olive x

In August 1967, Olive managed to get away for a week-long break. I took her to Oughterard, Co. Galway, where we stayed with my sister Kay and her husband, Dick Cotter. We explored Connemara each day, and so began Olive's love affair with the West of Ireland. That Friday, we drove across magnificent wild countryside to the quaintly named Loughnafooey (I have since been told it means 'the lake of the winnowing winds'). The view was breathtaking. Olive was, typically, concerned for a howling dog that was locked out of a cottage down below us. We kissed. I looked into her beautiful blue eyes and asked her the question that seemed so obvious: 'Will you marry me?' Without a moment's hesitation, she said, 'Yes.' There had been no plan. It just happened spontaneously. I was deliriously happy – delirious to the point of seeing three beautiful eyes in her face for the next hour! It was a perfect evening. We had come a long, long way from the first swab-test meeting.

Waterford,
October 1967

My dearest John,
Our sojourn in Waterford is proving most enjoyable and Daddy is thrilled with himself. He is attending two Masses every day, has joined the Third Order and has bought a booklet with the title, 'How to escape Purgatory'! Needless to comment, I am having a marvellous time teasing him – no hope for me, I'm afraid!

Your letter has just arrived and has made me all excited and all sad too. Me misses you terribly and loves you so much. What a complaint but how I enjoy it – particularly when we are together …
Not to worry, 'Christmas is coming' (I hope!) and the goose is getting fat, etc. Have a horrible feeling I shouldn't have said that – I can just imagine some of your comments! Darling, you bring out the worst in me!

When we arrive home on Wednesday I will have to take care of Mother straight away, so it may not be possible for us to meet. She is bound to be excited, so the presence of another person would not help her. Hope you can make out what I'm trying to say – if you can, you are a marvel! All things considered, it would be better to leave our reunion until Saturday. It seems years away and I feel so lost without you – perhaps you might phone on Wednesday – it would be something to keep one going until Saturday.

Apologies for this dreadful effort. At the best of times, I am hopeless with the pen and at the moment I am not even properly awake! Need your kiss to wake me up! Hope you can make sense of all this jumble. Will make sure you understand one thing – me loves you.

Take care.
All my love,
Olive x

Olive's mother died a month before we became officially engaged in December 1967. I remember having to borrow money from my sister to buy the engagement ring. We may have been rich in love, but money was scarce! As a teacher, I was earning about £1,000 a year. We had no home planned, but we decided to begin married life in the West of Ireland.

In July 1968, Olive 'escaped' to Wales for a brief holiday with her brother Jack and his wife, Pam.

My darling Olive,
I'm almost afraid to write this because it might turn out depressing if I keep on telling you how lonely I am – but I must write because I so desperately want to be with you ...

I'm sitting in the garden. They tell me it's a beautiful day – sun shining, birds singing, etc. – but for me, no! I live under a big cloud (my mother says I have all the appearances of it!). Oh darling, I'm absolutely and utterly LOST without you – no duck was ever so much out of water! Inwardly I feel so happy for you that you have finally got away from it all and are having a well-deserved rest – but words, however numerous or profound, could never convey my loneliness or love for you at this moment.

When you left on the boat on Saturday, I distinctly felt a few heartstrings go! I stood watching for a half-hour till my eyes strained and I could see no more. All the time I talked to you, kept telling you I love you, prayed for you. Madness? No, just that special way of feeling. Pauline was here yesterday and read Mother's teacup, seeing a wedding and a christening – whereupon Mother looked at me and said, 'My God, has she gone to Wales to have it?' Isn't it terrible what they think of my pet??

I dreamt about you last night – you were back in my arms and it was mmm! – nice! So you see I'm with you all the time, pet, even in my sleeping hours. Oh for the time when I can sleep by your side. Won't it just be heaven to be married, to come home to you, to be able to relax with you and at the end of the day to be by your side, hold you and be so happy, content – and proud to have marvellous you as my wife. Oh my darling, how I long to hold you so close to me again and see those big dreamy eyes full of love, that cute nose, to feel the moistness of you lips on mine, the warmth of your breath on my ear, to whisper the same old words again and again, to feel the tenderness of your fingertips, to enjoy the sheer thrill of being close to you …

Take care of yourself, my darling. I keep praying for you that everything may be perfect for you and that you may have the happiest and most relaxing of holidays. Someday we'll smile at how broken-hearted we were for a fortnight apart! But right now it isn't funny – I am pining away, seriously. But my whole goal in life is your happiness and if you are happy I will gladly pine away.

Thinking of you all the time. Me loves you, is lost without you. Wales doesn't know how lucky it is!

All my love,
John x

Wales,
July 1968

My dearest John,
Thank you, darling, for your three beautiful letters. I read and re-read them to give me comfort in your physical absence.

I awake with thoughts of you in the morning and sleep with thoughts of you at night (that sounds a bit dodgy!). You travel with me all through the day and talk with me about all the things I see and feel. Yet, my darling, I'm lonely and wish you were here with me in person. Talk about wanting everything on the same plate!!

Today is beautiful and I am sitting out in the sun writing this letter. The surroundings here are all you and I would ever ask for. You would love it here – mountains all around with sheep grazing on them and a stream running by the house. It is just awful that you are not here to share all this with me. Pam and Jack are so good to me. We are taking a picnic to the sea shortly – hence the usual rushed ending to this missive! Anyhow it's all your fault – I keep dreaming about you instead of putting my dreams on paper. It's a case of 'if I thought less I could write more'!

My darling, I love you so much that anything outside this love is a vague and nebulous thing. My love for you colours all my world so all things are beautiful. Will be home by boat on the 13th – the thought of seeing you on the quay has made me feel all excited! Must away – me loves and misses you very much.

All my love,
Olive x

On Wednesday, 18th September 1968, we were married in Trim, Co. Meath, where Olive's uncle was parish priest. The ring I slipped on Olive's finger bore the inscription *haec olim meminisse iuvabit*, the Virgil quotation that had come to mind on the day of our 'daring' walk in the woods of Blanchardstown. At the wedding reception I sang the song 'Try to Remember' with the lines 'when you were a tender and callow fellow'. Indeed I was, but I was also the luckiest and proudest fellow. This beautiful, beautiful woman, this vision in a black leather coat, had just promised all of her love and all of her life to me.

True to form, I had written a letter to Olive, to be opened on her wedding morning …

My darling Olive,
I know you won't have the time or the powers of concentration to read mail on your wedding morning, but maybe you will spare a minute for a faithful correspondent of the last two-and-a-half years!

The only reason I write is to give you a little giggle, to ease the tension, to make you happy. Come to think of it, that's the only reason I ever had for writing – and, in fact, the reason why I want you to accompany me down the aisle this morning. I'd look a right eejit on my own, wouldn't I? (P.S. You will turn up, won't you???)

As you read this, everything will probably seem in chaos, but a few hours will prove how worthwhile it all was. I know everything will be perfect, pet, so not to worry. I know more than anyone else how much you have done – all practically on your own – and how much you've gone through, and I admire and love you madly for it. So these last few hours – this storm before the calm! – must not upset you. I'm with you every moment and I'm going to be the proudest man there is to take you from your father after those forty-three paces up the aisle (I've counted them!).

This is your day, my darling. Sail through it with all the radiance that only you can show. This is the day we dreamed of – let us live that dream. Me loves you, my beautiful one. Me awaits you to make you my wife, to make you happy, happier than you know from here on. This is a historic missive – my last to you in our single state! We've come a long way, pet, but from here on the way is pleasant and paved with love. Come to me, my darling. Come.

John xxx

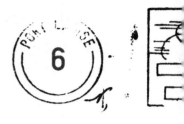

Into the West (1)

After all the traumas of the preceding two years (the Blanchardstown experience, Olive's operation, each of us losing a parent), we decided it would be good to escape to the West of Ireland for a while. I took a position as a secondary school teacher in Benada Abbey, a co-educational school with an orphanage attached, in the heart of the Sligo countryside, run by the Irish Sisters of Charity. We rented a cottage on the shore of Lough Talt – an idyllic honeymoon setting!

The first year of marriage was wonderful, of course – we were free to be ourselves at last – but it brought its own difficulties, as it must for all couples. Adjusting from the single life to a life of sharing takes time. On top of that, teaching at second level was a new experience for me and it required a lot of preparation. I was also expected to be involved in extracurricular activities such as football coaching, inter-school debates and the compilation of the school magazine. If that were not enough, I was persuaded to join the local dramatic group. My brief acting career extended to playing the role of Tuppenny Hayes in the Aclare Dramatic Society's production of M. J. Molloy's *Daughter from Over the Water*.

Olive was concerned for her widowed father and made a number of trips home to look after him. The year was further disrupted by a two-week strike by secondary teachers. Despite the fractured nature of our first year, we enjoyed our time in Sligo, and were made feel welcome by our neighbours and fellow-teachers. We took a particular interest in the twenty or so orphans (all girls) who had a difficult life, with little on offer to brighten their days in Benada. On a memorable spring afternoon,

Olive had a large group of them for tea in our little cottage. They were such lovable youngsters, craving affection and attention. They were so excited to have an afternoon of freedom, gabbing away, wolfing down sandwiches and cake, and smuggling women's magazines under their jumpers back to the orphanage.

It was an enjoyable year, but two events in the spring of 1969 brought a decision to return to Co. Meath. I was offered a position in St Patrick's Classical School in Navan. Taking that position would enable Olive to be near her father, and be spared the long trips up and down from Sligo. As it happened, she was in no position to be making those trips. She was pregnant. So, at the end of the school year, we bade farewell to Benada and set off for Navan with a small truckload of our still few possessions. I spent the summer correcting Intermediate Certificate English examination papers (a soul-destroying job) and supervising in the Gaeltacht school in Gibbstown – all in an effort to boost my meagre teacher's salary. With the help of an understanding bank manager and Olive's father as guarantor, we purchased a site and built a four-bedroomed bungalow a mile outside Navan – for what seemed the exorbitant price of just under £5,000.

While I was in Gibbstown, Olive stayed with her sister, Barbara, in Portlaoise.

Portlaoise,
Tuesday, 8th July 1969

My dear John,
Thank you for your precious missive. Our enforced separation is very hard to bear at times but dwelling on it only makes things worse. We will just have to take each day as it comes. Remember the motto on my wedding ring! Also we will have a wonderful time making up for our absence from each other – won't we?

My stay here is progressing along the lines that you would think most suitable! I am going to bed at a reasonable hour and I take Mark for a daily walk. My quality of sleep is mixed but could be worse. My nightly scratch is sorely missed – so are 'other things'! What is she talking about? Despite these drawbacks I am managing

*to enjoy myself in a quiet fashion. Barbara and I chatter away ad lib
to each other.*

*I don't envy you your job with the boys from Dublin – I imagine
they could be very entertaining! Don't forget to see Fr Walsh about
the job in St Patrick's – and about the flat. Aren't I mean issuing
orders to my poor, overworked husband? 'Tis a hard wife you have
landed yourself with!*

*Apart from my fainting episode at Mass last Sunday, 'it' is
behaving itself very well, thank God. As promised, I have no
intention of going to Mass this coming Sunday. You will have to do
all the praying for me.*

*Please write whenever you have a spare moment. Remember to
take your tonic and have as few late nights as possible. Me loves you
– madly!*

*All my love,
Olive x*

And on 4th October 1969, our happiness was multiplied by the
arrival of Elizabeth Emer Quinn – whom we would know and
love as Lisa. When I visited Olive that day in the Lourdes
Hospital, she was positively glowing in the radiance of
motherhood. I was so proud of her. And her first question to me?
'When can we have another one?'

I came home from the hospital and – of course! – immediately
wrote to Olive.

*Lonelyville, Navan!
Sunday night,
October 1969*

*My darling,
Seeing as how I won't be with you tomorrow, I must drop you a few
lines which you will have on Tuesday morning, D.V.*

*It was beautiful having that short time together this evening,
when I could release some of the feelings welling up inside me. Long
for your homecoming, when the floodgates will really open!*

Me is so proud of you, loves you beyond words, beyond any human power of description. So why try? If I didn't try, I would crack up altogether. And, of course, you would have to go and look a million and a half times more beautiful! You have no mercy on me at all! Result – I am totally immersed in you and Lisa. Love you, love you, breathe you, dream you. You are my whole life, the meaning and purpose of my existence – especially now when you have given me this wonderful gift, this treasure of treasures, this little soul for God.

Thank you, my darling, for everything – for Lisa, for being so wonderful about everything. Thank you, my God, for her. You knew what you were doing! Help me to be worthy of her. Rest and sleep, my beautiful one. I'll be with you very soon.

All my love,
John x

7

Goodbye, Mr Chips!

The arrival of a baby brings further adjustment to a couple's life – the baby simply takes over! Lisa took a few months to settle and, initially, had a lot of digestion problems. At the time, it was trying and seemed to be never-ending, but we coped.

Adjustment was needed in school also. Teaching in an urban, boys-only school was very different to a rural co-educational scene. I seem to remember a particularly lively class of first years, among whom was a cocky twelve-year-old called Colm O'Rourke who, many years later, would become my football hero! I remember an English class when we were discussing Spoonerisms and having fun with boys' names – Tony Booth became Bony Tooth, for example. I am almost certain it was O'Rourke who languidly raised his long arm and suggested – 'Sir, what about Seán White?' End of Spoonerisms! Nearly the end of young O'Rourke!

My teaching career ended in 1970 when I was approached by the educational publishers, CJ Fallon, and was offered the position of General Editor. I was attracted by the nature of the job, but even more so by the salary offered – £2,000 per annum (incredibly, almost twice my salary as a teacher) and eventually a company car. It was too good an offer to refuse. It would mean commuting daily to Dublin – common now, but not so in 1970 – and thus a long day for Olive with a very young baby, but she coped well. Olive always coped. The job change helped ease our financial problems, but money was always tight. We hadn't much of a social life. All through our married life, it was a matter of regret to me that I could not offer Olive a better life financially.

We always seemed to be scraping by. It wasn't that she expected or demanded better – quite the contrary – but I just felt she deserved better, and I would have loved to have been able to provide that 'better'. In hindsight, others could have provided better, but they wouldn't have loved her as much. What I could and did do for her was to ease her work burden and care for the children (something I enjoyed doing). That was the deal, anyway. In the courting days, in the flush of young love, I had promised to 'spoil' her, so why not spoil her in the most practical ways?

Thirty-one years later, broken by her absence, I would resume writing to Olive ...

Otterbrook, Galway,
11.43 p.m.,
Thursday, 26th July 2001

My darling,
There's nothing else for it but to start writing to you again after a 33-year break! Pardon the long delay ... Re-reading your wonderfully witty, clever and loving letters of 35 years ago I am just totally, madly, crazily in love with you all over again. (You rogue! – I had forgotten how well – and often – you wrote.) I love you. I love you, my beautiful one. I feel exactly as I did when I first read those letters of ours so long ago. Am I being a hypocrite? Am I just clinging to the past? No. No. A thousand times no. I want to believe and do believe this is all your doing. In the background Johnny Mathis is singing:

> What'll I do with just a photograph
> To tell my troubles to?

What'll I do, indeed? I need you so desperately. Please stay with me. Don't ever leave me again. Please protect me. Please. Please. Please. I just want to know that you're happy and you're here! There too – wherever, whatever that is.
I'm madly preparing for your party, because that's what you wanted, and that's what you shall have. Poor John Joe Quinn came

in earlier with a Mass card and stayed for coffee and at least five cigarettes. 'Ah Jeez, she was awful fond of this place.' And they were awful fond of you.

By the way, I love you. Did I mention that? Your photos are on display all over the place, I know you'll be mortified, but I want everyone to see them, and talk about you, and say how beautiful you were. This time 25 years ago, you were in the throes of labour, giving birth to our beautiful son. Thank you for him. He misses you greatly too. Please help him.

Your letters are a wonderful source of consolation to me. They recapture that time so well – innocence, discovery, tenderness, unfolding love. Read one today where you gave me instructions on how to get to your home in Stackallen. My first visit! I was so nervous. No wonder your father considered me a 'one hundred to one shot'. I think he thought I was one of your 'lost causes' ... The letter is postmarked 4/10/1966. Exactly three years later you would give birth to Lisa. Were we fast movers, or what?

Johnny Mathis is now singing 'My One and Only Love'. You were. You were. You were and you are, and you will be, my one and only love. It was a beautiful, beautiful love story, and nothing can ever change that. We went off the rails, or ran on different tracks latterly, and I so much regret that now. Please forgive me for all my stupidity, and please stay with me now, and always. Need you so badly. Love you. Love you. Love you. Stay. Please, please stay. Be all about me. Miss you so terribly.

All my love,
J x

More spoiling was needed in May 1972 with the arrival of Deirdre Quinn. To give birth to two children, and to care for them with the limitation of one lung, was no easy feat for Olive, but she managed it and managed to grow more beautiful in doing it. All of this, despite lifelong problems with sleep deprivation and, of course, when you have an invisible handicap like a missing lung, you often get little in the way of sympathy and understanding. Occasionally I would be guilty in this respect myself. *[You shouldn't have looked so beautiful, love.]*

Despite her isolation with two small children, Olive managed to forge a social life of her own, through liaison with other young mothers in the area. She took up golf for a while, and became involved in politics, acting as secretary to the Fine Gael branch. (Politics was in her blood – her father was a first cousin of the former Taoiseach, John A. Costello.) She loved the cut and thrust of local politics, and would come home from meetings to regale me with stories of the antics of local councillors. World politics would also impinge on our lives, however. The oil crisis of the mid-1970s sent petrol prices rocketing and, suddenly, commuting to Dublin became very expensive, even with the experiment of car-pooling. Reluctantly, we began to contemplate leaving Navan. Circumstances in my employment soon made that move a reality.

2.35 a.m.,
Sunday, 29th July 2001,
In bed – exhausted!

My darling,
The young ones are still partying below, but the rest of us have collapsed! O my darling, what a day! Did you enjoy it? Let me know – please. A wonderful, bittersweet day. Beautiful Mass. Aiveen and her singers carried out all your wishes – 'Amazing Grace', 'Ag Críost an Síol', 'Like the Deer', 'Be Not Afraid' – I did the reading, and spoke about your love for Killeenaran. It was more difficult than at the Funeral Mass, but I got through. Then down to Bernie's pub for 'a drink for Olive'. Back to prepare for the party. The food! All your women friends came up trumps again. You would – correction, did – love it. I know. I sang 'Try to Remember' – our wedding-day song – for my lost bride, and we toasted the Champagne Lady with Cava. The singing was great, but poor Mary O'Toole just couldn't sing – she was too emotional about you. I gave it my best shot for you, poochens. I love you so very much. That's all I can repeat, like a mantra.
Listening to Shirley Bassey singing 'What are you doing the rest of your life?' Me too. What am I to do for the rest of my life, but cling

to you? I love you so very much. Totally exhausted. Totally in love with you. Night-night.

Guz x Guz x
John x

Babes in the Wood – Olive with her twin sisters, Barbara and Clare

Do I have to do this?

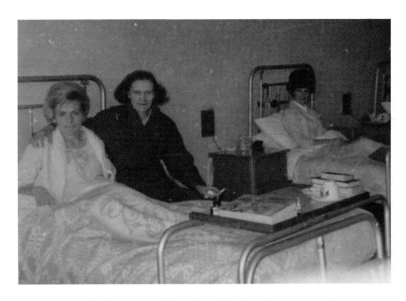

'The glamorous blonde in Ward 5' (see page 40)

'Down to the mortuary – exotic or what!' (see page 43)

Wedding day, 1968

The Black Leather Coat – in Greece

Our first home, Lough Talt, Sligo

With Lisa in Navan

Politics in the blood. With John A. Costello and his cousins, Olive's father and uncle, when Costello was given the Freedom of Dublin in 1975

All of us there, Greystones 1981

At the launch of Must Try Harder *(see page 101)*

What Lois Remembers (see page 106)

The Open Mind Guest Lecture 1998, University College Cork, with Helen Shaw, Director of Radio, RTÉ, and Senator George Mitchell

At the Jacobs Awards 1988

8

A Career in Broadcasting

At the end of January 1975, the hammer-blow landed. Fallon's informed me that they were terminating my employment. I was, in their view, not commercially oriented enough. As far as I was concerned, I had given my all to the best of my ability – overseeing the publication of as many as thirty new titles a year. I had to be master of all trades and subjects, from Leaving Certificate Technical Drawing to reading schemes for primary schools. That was the nub of the problem. I was stretched in too many directions. But I was proud of my work overall, and I had enjoyed my five years in publishing. If the Unfair Dismissals Act had been in force then, I would have taken Fallon's on, but I had no such avenue open to me. I was given a month's notice. No golden handshake. No handshake.

It took a while for reality to sink in. Here I was, with a wife, two young children and a mortgage – and I was unemployed, and without a car. I was so numbed by the experience that, on the day I handed back my company car, I made a phone call to my (very) understanding bank manager, and went straight out to buy a new car! I held my head high. I was proud of my work. But I was unemployed! A return to teaching was a possibility, but it might take time. Olive was, as ever, a rock of common-sense support. I had the feeling that something would turn up. And it did.

While serving out my notice, I noticed an advertisement for the position of Education Officer with RTÉ, part of a team behind a pilot schools radio service. Experience in education desirable. I applied, was called for interview and re-called for a second interview. An agonising wait followed during the month of

March – when I really was jobless – until eventually the letter of appointment arrived. We could breathe easily again.

Looking back, the Fallon's experience was a valuable part of my education. They may have deemed me a 'failure', but I never accepted that. And neither did Olive. It was part of life's experience and I was ready to move on to a new and different world.

Bray,
1.40 a.m.,
Wednesday, 1st August 2001

My darling,
Here I am – back again! I know I'm 'back again' – I mean back again in Bray! Via work, for which I had zero enthusiasm … Hated leaving the house. A tearful car-journey – dangerous for driving! Your photo beside me on the way.

Awake last night from 3.30. Finally made a 'tup of tea' and sat up reading the Blanchardstown Diary. Our first meeting on Easter Sunday 1966. So green (me!), so innocent, so tender, so beautiful (you!). It was a beautiful love story. The letters confirm it. And now … Now I'm racked with guilt. The last ten years. Coldness. Pride. Fucking stupidity. Ann Henning's poem haunts me:

> My love, when you die –
> If you die before me –
> I shall grieve …
> oh how I shall grieve
> for each moment of our life together
> that we had and did not treasure;
> precious gifts left unopened,
> blossoms trampled underfoot.
> Celebrations
> Lost forever.
> Sacrificed.
> Waylaid.
> Oh my love, how I shall mourn them.

Forgive me please. And be all about me. I'm so totally confused about the 'hereafter'. Doubts set in. What if – as you used to tease Derry – there were none? You must stay close to me, pet. If you don't, I'll just crumble. Feel so empty. Drained. Tired. To sleep, perchance to dream. How lovely it would be to dream of you. Night-night. Guz guz. Me loves you.

John x

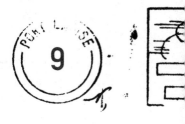

Into the West (2)

I joined RTÉ as an Education Officer on 7th April 1975. *Radio Scoile,* a ten-week schools radio project, was being piloted in primary schools in the Gaeltacht areas. I was assigned to the Connemara Gaeltacht to evaluate the programmes as they were broadcast, observe the children's reactions and the teachers' use of the programmes, talk with teachers and children and feed this evaluation back to the programme-makers in Montrose. Because of the length of the project, we decided to move *en famille* to the West for the duration. We rented a house in Oranmore. Little did we think that, sixteen years later, we would move permanently to another house eight miles down the road.

The work was interesting, and involved visiting schools all over Connemara and in the Erris peninsula in Mayo. Locating some of these schools, mostly one- or two-teacher schools, was a task in itself, but it was a joy to see the possibility that radio could offer children, particularly when they were in the care of an imaginative and enthusiastic teacher – sadly, not always the case. As for the Quinn family, they settled in very well in Oranmore. Lisa went to the primary school that was literally across the road. I remember a swarm of local children attending Deirdre's third birthday party, even though we were only a month in the place. And the weather was exceptionally good. It was a happy time. Olive and I enjoyed a good social life, and when we returned to Navan, only temporarily, at the end of June, we brought happy memories with us.

Commuting from Navan to Donnybrook (even in the 1970s) became increasingly problematic in terms of cost and time, and we reluctantly decided to put our first home on the market and move nearer to Dublin. We spent the spring and early summer of 1976 house-hunting, something which became a race against time, as Olive was pregnant again. In June, we finally decided on a three-bedroom bungalow with a large garden in Greystones, Co. Wicklow, and a month later, on 27th July, Declan John Quinn was born. Our family and our happiness were complete. (Regarding the former, I recently came across a birthday card from about that time which Olive had signed 'Love from Olive, Lisa, Deirdre and Declan. FULL STOP!') In August we moved house, always a traumatic event, leaving good friends and neighbours. In Olive's case, it was more difficult as, once again, she was moving away from the father she adored.

We had been blessed with three beautiful children. I was so proud of Olive and the way she coped with each birth and with the subsequent development of each child, given that she only had one lung. The years dim the memory, and it is only now, when I see Lisa coping with her baby, that I realise that once we had three children under seven, with all the attendant problems of illness, schooling, etc., and I say to Olive in daily chats with her: 'We were bloody brilliant!' And it was *we*. Even though this was before the advent of the 'New Man', I participated fully in the children's care and development, from nappy-changing to visits to the doctor. Seems (and should be) normal and natural now, but then it wasn't. I did it because I enjoyed it and because it was one of my ways of helping Olive through, one of my ways of loving her. I was always a practical lover! Olive didn't drive in those days, so I ferried her most places.

While the foundation of our marriage was solid, our relationship took the roller-coaster ride that I suspect most couples experience. Money – or lack of it – seemed to be a perennial problem. Doctor's bills and medication were constantly eroding any spare spending power we had. I always claimed I was entitled to shares in the local pharmacy, such was my contribution to its upkeep! As a result, our social life was diminished. I was never a pub person and, while we did get out for the occasional meal, Olive felt – justifiably – that she was deprived. She was very much a people person, and her main social outlets then were outings with female friends. It rankled with me then that I couldn't give her a better social life; it rankles even more in hindsight.

Things were not improved by events at work. The *Radio Scoile* pilot was deemed a success, but there was no government funding forthcoming for its expansion. The three education officers were maintained with research projects on various educational radio and television programmes. RTÉ encouraged me to pursue an MA in Education in University College Dublin, in order to extend my research skills. The MA was done by thesis and exam. It was the thesis part that nearly caused my undoing and a possible divorce! I decided to study children's leisure pursuits and was persuaded by a friend in the research business to do this by the 'diary method' – i.e. 1,000 children around the country would complete diaries (blocked out in half-hours) on how they spent their leisure time on a particular Tuesday, Thursday and Sunday in June 1977. Simple! Simple? Try reading 3,000 diaries and coding them for a computer under twenty different pursuit categories! I spent weeks – day and night – half-demented by this exercise. Olive was not amused! One of the few bonuses for her was that I could take a break from coding to give Declan his night-time feed!

Of all those diary entries, one stands out – a boy who simply wrote that his entire afternoon was taken up with 'firing stones'. Given that the stones were not aimed at a local glasshouse, I thought, 'What a wonderfully productive afternoon!' What dilemmas he must have been wrestling with! What solutions he must have (hopefully) come up with! I often cite this instance for the value of 'doing nothing' (as many of his peers wrote). But he and his peers did nothing for my marriage! I did get my MA and the friend who suggested the 'diary method' is still my friend. My future would not be in research, however. From the first day I walked into the Radio Centre in RTÉ, I knew what I wanted to do for the rest of my career. I wanted to be creating and making radio programmes.

Under a bough – à la your beloved Rubaiyat! – overlooking 'my field' in RTÉ,
4.46 p.m.,
Wednesday, 1st August 2001

My darling,
They call it 'my field' because I protested when it was converted to a car park. This year it has been returned to its field state! Fields ... I read a 1967 letter of yours this morning where you said that all the respite you needed from caring for your mother was to get out in the air – 'It was lovely to walk through the fields and think of you' ...

That touched me to the deep heart's core. Here I am, 34 years later, desperately looking for respite from my grief, getting out in the air, walking this field, thinking of you ... Clutching my little photo-album. Snatching glances from times past ...

I love you so much, my beautiful one. So very, very much. That's all I can say. All I need to say. And all I need to know is that you are here with me 'beneath the bough'. Rest your head on my shoulder. Give a little sigh of contentment. Love me. Lean on me. Never, never, never let me go.

John x

10

Making Radio

The opportunity to fulfil my dream came when Tom McArdle, one of the three original *Radio Scoile* producers, moved to television. I applied for the vacant radio producer position and was successful. It was the most important career move of my life. I knew I would love the job, and that's how it turned out. To be paid to do what I loved doing was a pleasant bonus. Ironically, Olive had doubts about my taking the job. She felt I would not be able for the criticism that would attend it! I was happy to prove her wrong in this instance.

Even more ironically, it was all her doing anyway! I have always felt that, if I had never met Olive, my life and career would have plodded on safely and predictably. I would have remained a reasonably good teacher, would possibly have been promoted to the position of principal, and would now be retiring from teaching not a little frustrated, cynical and tired! An okay life. But because I had met this beautiful, unusual and gifted woman, had fallen totally in love with her, and because she had seen in me the person she wanted to share her love and her life with, I walked through life with an inner confidence and belief in myself that would ultimately release the creativity I have enjoyed in my broadcasting and writing careers. It wasn't a case of her ever urging and driving me on (though she always said I should write – she knew I could write winning letters!), it was just the fact that I had won her heart that made me feel I could take up challenges other than teaching, and find my true niche. It may seem simplistic, but I know in my heart it is true. That is why I said to her in the radio programme *A Letter to Olive* (belatedly, I admit),

'You made me the person I am. My real date of birth was 1st March 1966. Throat-swab test. Vision in a black leather coat. Door closed in her face. Do I make myself clear?' It was the power of love and, of course, my regret is that I did not make myself clearer during our life together.

12.25 a.m.,
Friday, 3rd August 2001

My darling,
And still the letters come ... One from Chris Burke. Remember him? He remembers us being the first people to invite him to our home when he joined the teaching staff in St Patrick's in Navan. And a very touching letter from Colm O'Rourke whom I taught as a cheeky 12-year-old in St Patrick's and who went on to be my football idol ...

And now the doubts come. Strange, weird, frightening feeling tonight that you had 'wandered off' – your presence had 'evaporated'. Don't want this to happen. Read the Blanchardstown Diary, your scented letter, etc., but still had that feeling. Sat in the dark, listened to music, pleaded with you. I know you'll laugh but in my irrational, immature (what's new?) way, I wondered if you had met up with someone new! I can hear you laughing, but I'm in the depths. Feel alone. Cold. You can't have left me just like that. Is it your way (someone's way?) of telling me to pull back, 'get out of the past' rut, move on, as they say? Feel I failed you in so many ways over the last ten years. Should I leave these letters, stop writing those poems? No! Wrote a little poem called 'Trivia' today that pleases me, warms me.

Where are you, beautiful one? Please come back into my space. Please. In desperation I have put on a 1988 radio interview you did about Open Door ... Of course it seems as if you're here in the flesh – never went away. Unreal. (P.S. You were brilliant in the interview.) But it does draw you near – and it has cheered me up.

Before I go to bed – another card from my cousin Mary Frances. She quotes John O'Donohue – 'Grief is a journey that knows its way. Though travel is slow through the grief-journey, you will move through its grey valley and come out again into the meadow, where light, colour and promise await to embrace you.'

Will you be there to embrace me? And where are you now, my beautiful one? I want to love you. I want you. I need you. Hopefully a new day will bring you.

Guz x Guz x
John

TRIVIA

Let us talk of trivia –
Inconsequential
Insignificant
Half-remembered things.
What the children did
And said;
Characters we met,
The antics of a much-loved pet;
Our secret language
'The K is B …' (kettle's boiling!)
'I'd love a tup of tea …'
Nothing events
Like the note I left –
'I leaned against
The washing machine
And set it going …'
You laughed so much.
Like I said
Silly, inconsequential
Trivial things –
Things that bound us
Together,
Impenetrably …

I began life as a producer with *Radio Scoile*, which was still limping along with a limited service for secondary schools. I remember being totally in awe of Niall Tóibín as he read Frank O'Connor's story *First Confession* for a Junior English series. I had actually *produced* Niall Tóibín in my very first programme in my new role. Later that year (1977), I took over Tom McArdle's series *Knock at the Door* – a charming little programme which offered songs, rhymes, stories and things to do for the very young listener.

The very week I took it over was clouded for Olive and myself. Her father – the man who claimed I was a 'one hundred to one shot' in the courtship stakes (and he was right) – died at his home in Stackallen. A part of both our lives had ended, but for Olive the loss was enormous, such was the love she had for 'Bert'.

11

Radio Days and Holidays

My career in radio gathered pace as I grew in confidence and experience with the medium. The great thing about working in the Education Department (as it was then) was that, under its head, Maev Conway-Piskorski (whose father had taught me in primary school), you were given time to work on projects. Unlike the treadmill of current-affairs programmes and chat shows, education programmes were subject to careful planning and piloting, and I think it showed in the finished products. The range of subjects was quite broad, and if you had an interest or expertise in a particular area, you were encouraged to exploit it. Over the next few years, I moved from a children's magazine programme, *Alphabet* (whatever happened to children's radio?), through *I Remember, I Remember* (a series of interviews on childhood) to two important series for parents – *Learning to Read* (how parents can help the pre-reading child) and *Children Reading* (a parents' guide to children's leisure reading). The first interview I ever did was the pilot for *I Remember, I Remember*. My guest was Seán MacBride, and I listened with fascination as he recalled, in his beguiling French accent, how, as a boy, he flew kites with W. B. Yeats on a Normandy beach, or was treated to stories and ice-cream in a Parisian tea-shop by the writer James Stephens. This was *work?*

I was bursting with ideas for radio. It consumed my working life. Olive always claimed I was a workaholic. I always rejected that, on two counts. Firstly, I detest the word as it is not a word, but an example of the bastardisation of a beautiful language. Secondly, I disagreed, even in the accepted sense that she intended. I have never let my work dominate my life, or interfere with my duties as husband or father. I didn't bring my work home with me, as workaholics are often charged. Yes, ideas came to me during my home life – how I might structure this programme, approach that series, etc. As a radio producer, you are in the ideas business, and they came to me (thankfully) often unbidden and spontaneously, but they never became the addiction of workaholism (to use another non-word!). I simply loved my work, loved the challenges and possibilities it offered. In that sense, it wasn't work at all, more a hobby. I wasn't into other hobbies like golf or 'going out with the lads'. My other hobbies were simply home and family life and, because of the nature of my work, I could, and did, often work from home and structure my working day in ways that helped Olive. I was there to give her mornings off, bring the children to school, etc.

The rewards for all this love of work were simply the satisfaction of having made something worthwhile and the response of listeners. Occasionally, they went further than that. In 1981, I won the prestigious Governor of Tokyo Award at the Japan Prize (a major international competition for radio). It was for *The Miracle Tree* – a programme on language development in the young child. Whatever occasional friction there might have been about my 'workaholism', no one was more delighted with my success, or more proud of me, than Olive, and we celebrated in style. Other awards would follow over the years.

11.45 p.m.,
Sunday, 4th August 2001

My darling,
This morning, at an ungodly hour, you woke me with

Long ago and far away, I dreamed a dream one day
and now that dream is here beside me …

I sang that to you in our courting days, so you organise my waking to it now, don't you, pet? This is your way, isn't it? Your way of 'staying with me'. I want to stay with you, be with you. This may sound horrible in one way, but I really feel I have nothing else worthwhile to do here. The children could do without me, although I know they will say otherwise. Workwise, I've done all I wanted to do. Honestly, I would prefer to leave and be with you. I really, really would.

I spent the afternoon watching football on television, but this photograph beside me is haunting me.* I only found it recently. Where has it been all these years? Who took it? In some park? Before my time! You are so, so beautiful in it. I can't take my eyes off you and I can't bear to look at you! You are so beautiful. I have cried my way through two football matches – nothing to do with the football! – just repeating the mantra, I love you so very, very much. I cannot tell you often enough. It is beautiful and it is heartbreaking. My beautiful one. My one and only one.

I know you are in touch with me through this photograph. It's that look in those beautiful eyes. I love you. I love you. Want to be with you. Only you. You know that now. You must know it. I am so desperate. I need to talk this out with someone. I just love you so much. Can't take my eyes off that beautiful face. Stay with me. Haunt me – remember how you used to joke that if you went first, you would haunt me! Haunt me now, I beg you. I love you so very much.

What am I to do? What am I to do? I want to be with you – now and forever. I just love you so very, very much.

Guz x Guz x
John x

In that same year of 1981, we began our love affair with Rosslare. For six successive years, we rented a house there for the month of July. The only way we could afford this was to rent out our home in Greystones for the same period. There would be a big tidy-up at the end of June (why does your home never look better than when you are renting it out to complete strangers?). Then, on 1st

---

* This is the photograph used on the cover of this book.

July, we all squashed into the car with the dog, the two budgies, the tennis rackets, the sun-chairs (relics of the Papal visit) and the clothes, and the clothes. I know too well how Noah felt in the Ark, as we set off on that two-hour drive. (No, we are *not* going back for your favourite doll in the whole world!) They were very happy times – a wonderful closeness as a family, invariably good weather, freedom for the children – especially when we rented a little chalet which they dubbed 'The Little House on the Prairie' – and a special closeness for Olive and myself. No work ever intervened – well, just once when, in 1985, I had to come back to Greystones to interview Charles Handy for four hours on the future of work. It was the beginning of a long and fruitful friendship, and a dinner in Kelly's Hotel won Olive over all too readily.

What an irony that we would spend the last day of our holiday together in that hotel, and that Olive would die swimming in those same waters we had frolicked in. An irony? I think not. I like to think that, if she had the choice, Olive would have opted for the time, place and circumstances of her departure from this earth – happy, swimming in the Rosslare sea on a June evening while staying in Kelly's Hotel.

11.30 p.m.,
Sunday, 5th August 2001

My darling,
Here is the news.

1. *I love you so much. (That's news?)*
2. *Meath 2–12, Westmeath 3–9. They got out of jail again! Declan and I aged several years in Croke Park, but we squeezed out a draw. You certainly would not have been able to watch it and would have been 'all a tingle', as you wrote many years ago.*
3. *I love you so very much.*
4. *Declan is off the cigarettes and has rented a computer. I knew you'd like to hear that, but then you probably organised it!*
5. *I love you so very, very much …*

And your photo continues to haunt me – beautifully! I talk to you in the tenderest and most loving ways – like I did in the courting days (how quaint that expression seems today!). Why couldn't I talk to you like that in latter years? Don't know. I regret that I didn't make a better effort. Stupid. So stupid. Anyway, now it's like a damburst. The love and the tears flow – regularly. And you are here – I know that.

God, you were so beautiful! I really wasn't worthy of you. I thank you for becoming my wife and partner, and again I crave forgiveness for any hurt I caused you. I love you so very much. Am I boring you? I just love you – and it's beautiful, achingly, achingly beautiful.

Love, John x

12

Sunshine and Happiness

Olive's health became an increasing concern throughout the 1980s. In the spring of 1981, she was hospitalised with a lung infection that followed a bad flu – a very serious illness for someone with just one lung. A holiday in the sun was recommended. We scraped the money together and she went off to the Algarve in March with her sister Joan. I didn't go, because we couldn't afford it, the children were still at school and, anyway, I am not a sun person. It gave me time to reflect. I kept an occasional diary in those days and, on St Patrick's Day 1981, I wrote:

I really miss Olive, for all we differ and clash and irritate. There is no one like her and I love her ... so.

'There is no one like her'! How those words scream at me now! Sometimes it takes an enforced absence to make you see the obvious. Of course we argued, and had differing opinions and, at times, irritated the hell out of one another. But deep down, there was no one like her. That is what attracted me to her in the first place. That is what caused me to fall in love with her – her values, her gentleness, her kindness, her concern for others and, of course, her stunning beauty, which for me only reflected the beauty within. An enforced absence of two weeks brought me to my senses then. An enforced absence of however many years rifles it into my brain now. There is, was and will be no one like her for me. Get that into your head, you silly man, and be glad you had her presence, however fraught at times, for thirty-three years.

Olive came back from the Algarve that March looking a million dollars and feeling a million dollars. If only we had a fraction of a million dollars to send her there every year! We didn't, but we scraped together enough, somehow, to send her to the sun for the next twelve years or so. Mostly to the Algarve, sometimes to Spain, usually in the autumn to boost her strength for winter. Two weeks – sometimes three, if there were bargains going – usually with a girlfriend, but on a number of occasions on her own. I know family and work colleagues often raised an eyebrow at the latter, and probably thought dark thoughts, but we were just being practical and *trustful*. I had already used up my annual holidays, the children were back at school, and anyhow we simply could not afford to go away together. So Olive enjoyed the sun and I enjoyed my work. We were not being madly liberal at all. I wanted Olive to be strong and healthy and therefore happy and, on those grounds, the sun holiday worked. We weren't *that* kind of couple at all. *[Were we, dear?]* Come to think of it, that's all I ever wanted for Olive – to be happy. I know I had funny ways of showing it at times, but that was the goal. Beginning and end of story.

Diary of a Lost Soul
[Excerpts from a 1983 diary kept while Olive was on holiday in Portugal, recovering from illness]

Day 1: Well we waved to you as you took off. (Did you see us?) I can't remember having tears in my eyes saying goodbye to you going on holiday before ... brought the children to see *E.T.* (more tears!) and then to Granny's for tea ... Just now I pray you're sleeping, ready to wake to healing sun and air. And I miss you. And I love you.
P.S. As I was washing dishes in Granny's I thought of the mop you brought to apply suntan oil to your back ...
P.P.S. Who's the mopper?

Day 3: Cold and wintry. So am I. I see you're 'fair and hot'! Did you need the mop yet? I think of you a lot – and say a little prayer. Night Night!

Day 4: Bin day! Joy of joys! Still cold and showery. John Kennedy of JWT tells me the weather in the Algarve is fabulous. Hope you're enjoying every second of it. The mop? I wonder who's mopping her now ... Lisa made beautiful lemon custard tarts. Deirdre [*age 10*] made trouble ...

Day 5: Got official confirmation of Senior Producer Grade today. You certainly picked the right week to go away – winter is still here. And all I've got is a hot-water bottle. And all you've got is a mop! That's what worries me ...

Day 8: I hope you didn't try to ring us as Lisa was tricking with the phone – ringing the talking clock. Result – the line is jammed and every time we lift the phone we get – 'At the signal ... ' Drive you round the bend. Had difficulty persuading Deirdre to go to Mass today. She doesn't 'understand' Mass and finds it boring ... I was particularly lonely for you today. Don't know why – just thought you might like to know. Think about that while you're being mopped ...

Day 9: Hooray! The talking clock is gone! Boo! The rain is back! I see you were only 'Fair and 64°' – hope you're not depressed too. No post from Portugal yet ... I'll have to post this today.

Guz x Guz x. Be good – and if you can't, be careful who you give the mop to! Miss you. Love you. Please get better. And strong. And madly passionate. Come home and devour me!

Love, John x

The trouble with happiness and its pursuit is that life keeps getting in the way. We hope for the best. We hopefully try our best, but the vicissitudes of life conspire to frustrate and thwart us. In our Blanchardstown days, Olive would write witty 'postmarks' on the envelopes of her letters. I remember one of them which summed up Olive's frustrations – 'No postman! Now rain! Life!!'

85

These simple frustrations would be writ large in our married life. Of course there were happy times, very happy times – the photograph album is as good a book of evidence as any – but life, married life, is really about coping with the down days, the 'typical ould Mondays' (to quote James Plunkett) when things go wrong, the boring days when nothing much happens, the 'deep freeze' days when opinions don't so much differ as clash violently, the moody days, the days of illness, the days of hurt, the days you would want to forget. Every relationship has them, but doesn't always admit to them. All you can do is try to get through them, around them, over them. Sometimes you succeed, sometimes you don't try hard enough, sometimes you just run away.

Now, of course, I can see those 'down days' in true perspective, and so many of them were so ridiculously trite, and we were both so silly not to see them as such, but then they were so big, so insurmountable. We humans are a strange, strange species! And, of course, hindsight brings regrets, big-time regrets. A stupid, stupid occupation, I know, but who doesn't fall foul of it now and again? I am comforted by a neighbour in Galway in this regard. 'I have no time for this regret stuff,' she says. 'If you didn't travel the road you travelled, you wouldn't be where you are now!' Very Irish, but very true. It is the path you take in life that makes you the person you are. Given my total and complete love for Olive now, the road we took was worth all the potholes and wrong turnings. *[I just hope you feel the same, love. Someday we'll sort it all out! In the meantime, I am sorry for all the time I didn't try – and yes, dear, I know I could be trying at times!]*

11.15 p.m.,
Monday, 6th August 2001

My darling,
Just back from a live radio production of The Tempest. *Brilliant! 'Chaos becomes order through magic, forgiveness and love.' I'll drink to that!*

Prior to that I went to see Mary Magee. What a wise and inspirational woman at 92! In five words she unlocked my troubled mind – 'Heaven is nearer than Galway.' She went on – 'Olive is with you now all the time, loving you, all-knowing. You are closer now to each other than ever.' It is so. I know it. Feel it. She was such a consolation.

As was Anam Chara *when I read it this morning. 'Pascal says, "In difficult times you should always keep something beautiful in your heart." Perhaps, as a poet said, it is beauty that will save us in the end.' Indeed. And beauty is truth ... And in our case, the something beautiful is you, my love, and our beautiful, gentle, tender love. Of that I am convinced, my darling.*

If that wasn't enough, we had Lyric FM all day with its 100 most requested pieces of music. Sheer joy! Thank God for Lyric and for music. And you, of course, are the music. Stay very close to me, my beautiful one. As Prospero reminds us:

> We are such stuff as dreams are made on
> And our little life is rounded with a sleep.

Love you always,
John x

13

The Open Door

Sometime late in 1982, Clare Dunphy knocked at our door. Clare was the local public health nurse and she lived just around the corner from us in Greystones. She knocked on the door with a purpose.

In her daily work, Clare was coming across an increasing number of physically disabled adults who were prisoners in their own homes. They had no social outlets, no opportunities to develop their talents, to be the people they could be. This wasn't right, Clare thought. To compound matters, the disabled were being cared for day in, day out – and night in, night out – by devoted partners, parents or family members (who, in many instances, had given up their careers to care for their loved ones). Equally, the carers were very often prisoners – willing prisoners, but prisoners nonetheless. This certainly wasn't right, Clare thought. The system was failing these people. She voiced her opinions but nobody was listening. 'We need someone who is political, someone who will kick up a fuss,' she said to a friend. 'I'll try Olive Quinn!' She obviously knew Olive Quinn better than most, and when Olive opened the door to Clare that day, it was a symbolic beginning to a quite extraordinary adventure.

As a child and as a young woman, Olive was always teased by her family as being the 'Patron of Lost Causes'. If there was a 'lame duck' or a down-and-out in the vicinity, Olive would be the one who would show practical concern for that person – an alcoholic, a Traveller, a homeless person, a beaten wife – 'oh, another of Olive's lost causes', they would say. Scoff they might – and we all occasionally scoffed – but Olive had a fierce sense of justice. She

89

simply could not understand, and would not tolerate, injustice in any form, and refused to walk away from it. Of course, we could be embarrassed by all of this. 'Look, don't get involved,' we would say. 'Not our business. The government's fault. Leave it. You'll get yourself into a mess. And what about your own health?' All the excuses we could muster for our own inadequacy, our guilt. They cut no ice with Olive, and only made her more determined. Once she got her teeth into injustice, she was the proverbial terrier. Would not let go. Oh, she was 'political' all right. Clare Dunphy had chosen well.

The test case that Clare outlined that day concerned Helen Clarke. Helen was the only child of Kevin and Phyl Clarke and, at the age of twenty-one, with a wonderful life before her, she developed a brain tumour which paralysed her and left her with a life of quiet desperation in a wheelchair. Kevin, a recovering alcoholic, had to continue working, to maintain his family. Phyl was frail and arthritic. A desperate situation. Olive went to visit them and the Clarke family subsequently became good friends of ours. More importantly, she was convinced about Clare Dunphy's argument. There were other Helen Clarkes about. A centre was needed to provide care and development for the disabled on a daily basis, and, equally, to give respite to their home-carers. And so the struggle began.

11.20 p.m.,
Tuesday, 7th August 2001
(My mother's 99th birthday!)

My darling,
Three most extraordinary things to tell you about. You know already, but I'm telling you anyway!

1. *Went from work into town on the bus. Declan happened to be on the same bus! We spent the journey going through my mini photo album of you. He is such a lovely lad – everyone says it. There is so much of you in him. What other 25-year-old would stand there in D'Olier Street and kiss his father goodbye?*

2. *Decided to walk back to RTÉ for the exercise. (Who's good?)*
Coming through St Stephen's Green, I remembered a glorious
autumn day last year when we sat on a bench in the Green and
just enjoyed the contentment of it. In memory of that I sat down
for a smoke and was actually leafing through the photo album
(again!) when I was accosted by a down-and-out – one of the
three guys who were lying on the grass across from me. 'Any
chance of an ould cigar, boss?' says he. I gave him one, hoping he
would go away, but instead he sat beside me, lit up and told me
his story. A former jockey who had ridden for all the big names.
Threw a few races, was brought before the stewards and lost his
licence. Everything went downhill from there. Hit the bottle,
marriage broke up and here he was living rough, on the touch in
Stephen's Green. He was a really likable guy – witty and
articulate. ('I have no intention of leaving this planet just yet.')
You would have enjoyed him – one of your 'lost causes'. I gave
him a few bob and got up to leave. For some reason, I told him I
lost you a month or so ago. He embraced me (I can hear you
laughing!), leaned forward and whispered in my ear:

The seed in your heart shall blossom …

Just that. Extraordinary! Weird! Wonderful! He stunned me initially.
When I looked back he gave a little wave and mimed the message
again – 'The seed in your heart shall blossom.' Poetry! Quite beautiful
really. It was you surely? It could only have been you. Thank you.
3. *Later, listening closely to your favourite ABBA song, the words*
jump out –

When the time is right
I'll cross the stream
I have a dream
I believe in angels

Are you talking to me or what?

Love, John x

91

The initial response from the health board was disappointingly predictable. The numbers weren't there to justify a day centre. A handful of people, they said. Olive joined forces with a friend, Mary Hackett, and with Pádraigín Hughes, whose husband was disabled. They did their own research, carried out their own census, travelling the highways and byways of North Wicklow. The 'handful of people' grew to thirty, forty, maybe more. The three women made their case and continued to lobby. They enlisted the support of Monsignor John O'Connell, the dynamic parish priest of Holy Redeemer Parish in Bray, a parish noted for its range of innovative social services. He, in turn, enlisted the help of prominent businessmen in the town who would act as trustees for the project. The wheels were turning.

Olive was in her element now. The politician in her revelled in a challenge. This was not charitable work, in her view. It was simply a matter of rights, of justice. The physically disabled and their carers had been 'lost causes', but their patron had arrived, and woe betide the authorities who took her on! The project needed a name. Olive came up with one. Open Door. A symbol for inclusiveness, for welcome. The disabled would not be 'patients' or 'clients'. They would be *members* of a warm, embracing community. Olive threw her energy and time totally and willingly into Open Door. Her energy was limited, given her health problems, but it was never a disadvantage. She had the time. The children were all at school and, while they now recall Mum being almost constantly on the telephone (we won't talk about the phone bills), when they came home from school they were always her first concern. And the husband? Well, he was good at writing letters, remember? So he wrote letters (willingly) to ministers, health board personnel, the Wheelchair Association. He wrote letters.

It all came to fruition in December 1984, when agreement was reached and the Open Door Day Centre for the Physically Disabled opened in temporary premises in Fatima House, a Legion of Mary hall in Bray. The beginnings were rudimentary – six members and a staff of three. The members were collected by ambulance and brought to a place where they could socialise, pursue interests and crafts, avail of physiotherapy and occupational therapy, and have a hot meal delivered daily from Loughlinstown Hospital. But from day one, what immediately impressed the visitor was the wonderful atmosphere of warmth, enjoyment and love that permeated the centre. I was so happy for the three women who had worked so hard, but I was immeasurably proud of Olive. She had proved that it *ought* to be done, it *could* be done – and now it was done. And Clare Dunphy had a knowing smile on her face …

11.40 p.m.,
Wednesday, 8th August 2001

My darling,
Lisa rang from London this morning to tell me that there was a tribute to you in The Irish Times! *Raced down to the newsagents mid-breakfast (only for you would I leave my breakfast!) and there you were – Pat Hunt's glowing appreciation – gloriously in the middle page of* The Times. *I cried with delight and pride. Love you to bits.*

Tim Kennedy from Open Door rang. He can't believe you're gone. You meant so much to him – he 'would follow you to hell and back'. I played my new CD of Tchaikovsky's 'Pathètique' Symphony just to savour your theme – the slow movement. It has always reminded me of you – elegant, languid, graceful. I read your hospital letter 'postmarked' No Postman! – Now Rain! – Life!! (How I loved those 'postmarks' of yours.) How brilliant you were! How wonderfully – and quickly – we fell in love: 'Nice to know we've tuned in on the same wavelength.'

And you appreciated my King Lear *quote:*

> No, no, no, no …
> We two alone will sing like birds i' th' cage …

I got as big a thrill reading it today as I did in 1966. I love you so very much. Please stay close to me. Lots of comments on your tribute, including a phone call from an upset Pádraig Mac Gréine, now in his 102nd year.

John x

P.S. I'm upset too. Please come and live in the cage with me.

APPRECIATION
OLIVE QUINN

The Nobel prize-winner Seamus Heaney paid an exquisite tribute to the late Olive Quinn, who will long be remembered for the key role she played in establishing the Open Door Day Care Centre in Bray.

Speaking at her graveside in Shanganagh cemetery, he picked up on some words of the liturgy of her Funeral Mass in the Church of the Most Holy Redeemer.

'Heaven,' he remarked, 'is one of the first words we become aware of in childhood.' Seamus observed that as we grow older the idea of heaven flourishes more in our minds than in images formed in childhood. How right he is. With the passing of time the names, images and personalities of loved ones gone to heaven populate and crowd our minds and memories.

Seamus recited his beautiful poem 'The Wishing Tree' at Olive's graveside.

In the poem he thinks about his recently deceased mother-in-law. 'I thought of her as the wishing tree that died/And saw it lifted root and branch to heaven.' The poem concludes: 'I had a vision/Of an airy branch-head rising through the damp cloud/Of turned-up faces where the tree had stood.'

Olive was a 'wishing tree' who fulfilled three great wishes: to love, to be loved, and to make life easier and happier for the physically handicapped and their families. Indeed, the olive tree possesses a wealth of symbolism: peace, fruitfulness, strength, victory and reward. All of these qualities Olive Quinn possessed, and more.

The Open Door Day Care Centre is the enduring manifestation of her love for her fellow human beings. How appropriate it was that three wheelchair-bound members of Open Door brought gifts to the altar before the Offertory of the Mass. Open Door is not just a haven; it is a heaven on earth for its members.

Many people and institutions worked long and hard to create it, but the initial idea was Olive's. In the early 1980s she developed the project with her friends Mary Hackett and Pádraigín Hughes.

Father John O'Connell PP arranged to make Fatima Hall available to them in 1984. An army of fundraisers, led by Joe Duggan and Jim Daly, joined the project, and in 1987 the Open Door facility moved to Boghall Road. The Department of Health, Eastern Health Board and the Wheelchair Association also played pivotal roles in its development. In 1994 Open Door moved to its present, purpose-built premises on Vevay Road, where more than eighty members enjoy its benefits.

Olive's commitment to her cause became legendary. During protracted negotiations she could talk entire delegations into submission to her will.

Never robust in health, she could use her delicate disposition to disarm and charm budget-conscious officials. Olive radiated style, personal and verbal, and had a dress sense that made her appear as royal as her native Co. Meath.

Openness and generosity of spirit are qualities we associate with Olive and her husband John Quinn. It is fitting that she founded Open Door and that John's programme on RTÉ Radio One is called *The Open Mind*.

Olive is in heaven now, no doubt bending the ear of God to make even more good things happen for the members of Open Door. May she enjoy her eternal reward.

The grateful people of North Wicklow extend their condolences and appreciation to John, and to their children, Lisa, Deirdre and Declan.

14

Keeping the Door Open

Opening the door was a difficult enough task. Keeping it open proved in many ways more arduous. The centre operated under the aegis of the Eastern Health Board, but the Open Door trustees were committed to raising a substantial level of funds each year to maintain its operation. Over the years there followed the succession of initiatives that every voluntary organisation must pursue in the never-ending quest for funds – Lord Mayor campaigns, fashion shows, Christmas Day swims, cheese-and-wine evenings, barbecues, concerts – we had them all. Soon after his first Eurovision win, Johnny Logan succumbed to Olive's charm and agreed to be the official starter to a sponsored bed-push from the GPO to Greystones! It was a particularly difficult time for local fundraising, as global issues, such as the Ethiopian famine, dominated. As well as competing with each other, many deserving local causes were also competing with Live Aid.

I made my own small contribution to Open Door by compiling and publishing a book called *Must Try Harder*, a collection of school memories from sixty well-known personalities. We sold about 5,000 copies at £5 per copy. It was done, as I said in the preface, 'with love and admiration for Olive'.

The centre was recognised as an outstanding success within a couple of years. This was reflected in its winning a Bray Civic Endeavour Award, but success brought its own problems. The growing membership, and the facilities they needed, put increased pressure on Fatima House. New premises were required. Olive was chairperson of the Board of Trustees and became involved in lengthy negotiations for a health and fitness club that became available on the Boghall Road in Bray. Open Door eventually moved there, but it was never an ideal location, being situated in the middle of an industrial complex. As it happened, Glaxo, the industrial giant next door, needed to expand its premises. The pressure was on Open Door to move again. More negotiations, on top of the quite considerable task of running a growing project, put a strain on the Board of Trustees, and especially on its chairperson. Olive relished the cut-and-thrust of the boardroom, but often became angry and frustrated when difficulties arose, internally and externally. She had a simple dream – that Open Door would be the best day-care centre there was, just because its members were entitled to that. She was perhaps naive at times, but her commitment to the success and growth of Open Door was total and unflinching. She would often come home from board meetings angry and frustrated that others could not agree with her point of view. She fought many battles. Not everyone saw things her way, but they could only admire her grit.

Midnight,
Thursday, 9th August 2001

My darling,
The things one thinks of … When did I first kiss you? Can't remember – sorry! – but I know it was beautiful and I'm certain I was in love with you before that.

Anyway – had a nice meal with Declan and Kelly tonight. They're a pair of dotes. We talked about you lots and I talked about you lots. Love you lots … Before that I went back for more consolation and wisdom to Mary Magee. The woman is a saint – there are no two ways about it. She talked of God perfecting our relationship. He didn't take you away. He just raised you to a higher plane. 'Olive's "Purgatory" is her edging closer and closer to God … you only ever wanted her to be happy, so now you must learn to accept that hers is the ultimate happiness. It will be painful – very painful – but she is closer now than ever. There is no physical separation – you in Dublin, she in Galway – anymore. She is with you. She knows.'

It is so. You are 'in the light'. Perpetual light. You know how much I love you. Miss you. Want to be with you. I'm still thinking of that down-and-out. 'The seed in your heart will blossom' … It will be so. Is so. Love you so much, much, much. Forever.

John x

Open Door eventually found its permanent home in October 1994, when a purpose-built centre was opened by the then Minister for Health, Brendan Howlin TD, on land acquired from the Loreto Sisters on Vevay Road, Bray. It continues to thrive, with a membership of eighty, a wonderfully dedicated staff – both paid and voluntary – and exceptional facilities, but, above all, it is permeated by that same atmosphere of warmth and love that filled Fatima House twenty years ago. With no disrespect to all who have worked for and in Open Door, it is Olive Quinn's lasting legacy to North Wicklow. I know I am biased, but I also know exactly how much Olive spent herself in pursuit of her dream. Everybody else saw the elegant and beautiful woman who presided at meetings and official functions, the tough unyielding negotiator, but only I saw the woman who suffered all her married life with sleep deprivation – often driven to the point of feeling almost suicidal. Only I shared with her the depressing prognosis her chest consultant delivered to her in the mid-1980s – her one lung was expanding to fill the vacuum in her chest cavity and, in doing so, was pulling and twisting her bronchial tubes, leaving her liable to repeated infection. Did she ever use these continuous health problems to gain sympathy, or to score a point at board level? Never. Did she ever look anything less than the proverbial 'million dollars' at any function or meeting? Never. I don't know how she did it. She was quite an extraordinary woman. There really was no one like her.

11.45 a.m.,
Saturday, 11th August 2001

My darling,
Just sitting here listening to the 'Romeo and Juliet Overture', gazing at your photo. You are so, so beautiful. The sheer radiance of your face. Is that how you 'look' now? I know that's stupid, but I still like to think so. I love you so terribly much – no arguments, ifs, buts, questions about it. More in love with you than ever. All your fault. Your beautiful fault.

Thought a lot on my way back from my morning walk. Can't believe my luck. How blessed I was that you replied to my first letter (written in German!) and to all the subsequent ones; that you wrote to me two or three times a week (you who hated writing) – often when you were in severe pain after that barbarous operation; that you slowly unfolded your beautiful nature to me; that you met me for our first date and then didn't say – 'well, you're a nice guy, but …'; that you continued to meet me and that we fell in love so beautifully and so rapidly; that you said 'yes' to me thirty-four years ago tomorrow in Connemara; that you agreed to give your love and your life to me, who was so raw and naive and immature but so, so, so very much in love with you. For all of that, my darling, I thank you with all my heart. Truly, I wasn't worthy. Truly. No bullshit. No false modesty. Truly.

No wonder I walked on air then! I really did! This is all pouring out of me, just like the tears. I loved you. I love you now more than ever. In between? Disgusted with myself over lost opportunities of the last ten years when we seemed to drift apart … I know I can't fix the past but I know I always did things for you. That was my way. Spoil you. Your first letters said how you loved being spoiled. So I spoiled you. Not enough. 'You spoiled her,' they said, making it sound like a crime. Why shouldn't I have spoiled you? That's what it was all about. Why didn't I say that to them? Why didn't I spoil you more? Especially latterly. Why? Why? I know you weren't 'yourself' in the last five years, but why? Why? Why?

Why am I pouring this out? Because I have to. Because I love you so much. This is tearing the guts out of me. I love you. I love you, my beautiful one, my only one. Thank you. Thank you. Thank you.

John x

On top of all that, Olive suffered severe whiplash injuries in a car crash in 1987. Her health problems seemed never-ending. 'They'll have to shoot me in the end, like they shoot horses,' she used to say. But she kept going. And because she always maintained her looks and her dress sense, no one knew what she was really going through. Except me.

I burst with pride whenever I walk through the Open Door Centre now – pride in someone who fought so hard and at considerable personal cost to realise her dream. When Olive died, I wanted to leave some lasting tribute to her in the centre. I found it in a photograph taken in RTÉ in 1985 at the launch by Pat Kenny of *Must Try Harder*. Olive is standing on a chair making her chairperson's speech (a thing she hated doing). I am holding her hand for moral and positional support. People are laughing. It is a wonderful photograph, taken by our friend Ray Flynn. I went back to Ray to have it enlarged. I then had it framed and presented it to Open Door. The caption says, 'I Have A Dream' (Olive's favourite ABBA song). Underneath I wrote that I chose the photograph for four reasons:

1. It was taken at an Open Door function.
2. Olive is making people happy – if you ignore Messrs Kenny and Quinn who are seriously perusing *their* speech notes.
3. Olive is head and shoulders above everyone else!
4. I am holding her hand!

Enough said …

Loughnaphooey,
Co. Galway,
4.28 p.m., Sunday, 12th August 2001

My darling, my darling, my darling,
Here I am thirty-four years later – almost to the minute – back in Loughnaphooey on a dreary, misty afternoon. Here on the most beautiful day of my life, I held you in my arms and asked you the only question I could ask you: 'Will you marry me?' And you said, 'Yes. Yes. Yes.' And I kissed you so tenderly and looked so lovingly on your beautiful, beautiful face. And you had three beautiful eyes – an extra one on your forehead! And I was so unbelievably happy. Unbelievably. And I loved you so indescribably much.

We looked down at a cottage on the riverbank where you were so concerned over the sheepdog who seemed to be locked out or abandoned. And I kissed you again and loved you even more. There was no plan. It was just you and the place and the moment. Never was a question so obvious. Never was an answer so immediate and so certain. Thank you so much, my beautiful darling. No regrets. I only delight in the memory of it all.

Now – the tears flow as freely as the mountain stream cascading down behind me. That photo sits on the steering wheel. You gaze at me, smiling, and you're saying Yes. Yes. Yes. I'm here, you're saying. I'm here, darling, and I love you too. That's what you're saying. Such a beautiful face. Such a beautiful place. My heart could – probably will – burst with joy. Why did we never come back here? Why? There are so many whys. Forget that now. We are here now. So close. So close. Your presence envelops me. And I am so, so happy. So lonely but so happy. So, so much in love with you.

The cottage is derelict now. No dog! The rain sheets across the valley. Your radiance shines through the gloom. Hold me now, my beautiful one. Hold me and keep saying yes, yes, yes. I will give my life and my love to you for all of that life – and beyond. Hold me. Love me. Stay with me. My beautiful three-eyed one. I love you so very, very much. That's all I can say. Want to say. Forever. And ever.

John x

15

Into the West (3)

By the end of the 1980s, Open Door was thriving. Olive loved the house in Greystones and we had good neighbours, but she was growing restless. She felt that Greystones lacked a sense of community. It was fine if you played golf or tennis, but if you weren't the sporting type? There were several voluntary associations (and Olive did have a brief dalliance with Fine Gael again), but somehow she never found the community sense that suited her – not that the Open Door left her with much time for any other commitments. Greystones was a fast-expanding dormitory town, but, for some reason, it was not offering her contentment. Maybe her health problems were greater than even I knew; maybe she was just tired and needed new pastures; maybe, most of all, she was just a country girl at heart.

When the country was going bananas over Ireland's exploits in the 1990 World Cup, we were on holiday in Spiddal, Co. Galway. The landscape and the people seemed to re-awaken something in Olive – a longing to be part of that landscape and people whose openness she responded to instantly. Another dream was forming in her head. Could we not live here in the West? I was initially sceptical, but Olive persisted. Of course, it was a romantic idea, but it could be done. I would still have to be based in Dublin, but there were regional studios in Galway and Limerick. I was tempted by the idea. It was not something we could have done when the children were small, particularly given Olive's health problems. Now the girls had flown the nest, and there was only Declan, who had started secondary school. The onus would really be on Olive, who would have to do without me for four or five days a week. Maybe that was a pleasing prospect for her! Who knows?

12.45 a.m.,
Thursday, 16th August 2001

My darling,
I begin to the strains of 'When I Fall in Love'. This has been a very difficult day. It began with my going through a diary from the 1970s – it brought home to me how I had failed you. Endless problems with money – debt, debt, debt – rows, no proper social life for you, my occasional 'misbehaviour'. How you had traipsed around with the children – to Navan, to Cork – to give them a holiday. What a miserable life you had then. I really let you down. I am so sorry.

Then to cap it all I came across a letter from the early 1990s about what was a misunderstanding over insurance money. You were so low, so unhappy – 'are there any fences left to mend?' … I destroyed the letter but it practically destroyed me. I went to Mass in Ballinderreen yesterday in abject and utter despair and regret, begging your forgiveness for all the hurt and what seems very little love. What was I at? What were we at? I am so, so sorry, my pet. Please forgive me. Please. I feel you have every right to just wander off 'out there' and be rid of me, but, please believe me, in my strange way, I did love you – and I do so love you now. I have to believe that you know that much now – now that you are 'in the light'. I love you so very, very much. I just want to start all over again.

All my 'achievements' – academic, my books, my radio productions, awards – seem pretty worthless right now. I feel so low, so rotten but so, so much in love with you. Crazed. I am absolutely terrified you will wander off on me. Called into your bank in Oranmore with your Death Certificate to close your account. Am I really doing this? I asked myself. The last straw …

Drove back to Dublin and then what awaited me? Letters from all over – the news of your death is only spreading now, thanks to Pat Hunt's obituary.

Some examples:

An absolutely beautiful, detailed letter from Cardinal Cahal Daly

> I did not have the privilege of knowing Olive but it's clear she was quite a wonderful lady ... she is still close to you ... and she has only gone as far as God and God is very near.

I am so proud of you – that a Cardinal should be moved to write about you.

Elizabeth Handy

> Although Charles and I never met Olive, I feel I almost know her, as you often spoke of her – and you were obviously a devoted couple.

Pegg Monahan

> Being without Olive is a very hard road to walk – and healing and peace come dropping very slow.

Edith Newman-Devlin

> *But true love is a durable fire*
> *In the mind ever burning*
> *Never sick, never old, never dead*
> *From itself never turning.*
> *(W. Raleigh)*

> What luck – out of all the women you could have met and married, to have chanced on someone with those lovely qualities.

It's true, so true. The letters go on – I almost burst open there at my desk, reading them. Little Angela Murphy from Presentation Radio who 'couldn't approach me in person' (one of many, I suspect) and who had been 'relentlessly' lighting candles for you.

Talk each day to Olive and she will help you.

I do. I do.

Lois Tobin (from the Lady Gregory Society)

I only met Olive with you at the spreading of Catherine Gregory's ashes at Coole Lake. She was so gracious and I recall you helping her over the steps and her smiling at you.

Isn't that just beautiful? Such a trivial thing, but remembered.

Doireann Ní Bhriain

It's a very long time since I met Olive but I have a vivid memory of her energy, dynamism and enthusiasm in her work with Open Door.

Tom Grealy

I am just someone who listens to you on the radio … I offer you my sympathy … What I read confirms how very special your wife was.

Karen, Anne and Sue (your hairdressers)

We were so shocked, it had taken us till now to write … Olive was such a charming, attractive, witty lady … she could exasperate you but it was only to achieve perfection! … she was so well read and loved to chat … we all miss her so much.

And so it goes. What mail to receive in one day! It broke my heart reading the letters but it lifted me too. I just love Lois Tobin's memory – it reminds me of your 1967 letter, 'it was lovely to walk through the fields and think of you'. O my beautiful one, if only I could rewrite the script … I know that's stupid but … I did, did, did love you – and love you even more now, now that the scales have been lifted from my eyes and the dam has burst in my heart. Please forgive me. Please, please, please stay with me. I need you so much. I feel I will break in two. I only have to look at that photo – Radiance, Radiance, Radiance. How beautiful you must be now in the 'perpetual light' … I couldn't be worthy but I need you so desperately. Snuggle in to me. Don't wander off. Stay. Stay. I love you – forever.

John x

It was a colour photograph in the property section of *The Irish Times* that initially caught our eye. A two-storey thatched house on the sea in South Galway – not an area we knew at all. We originally had Barna/Spiddal in mind. We went to see it – on a scorching, blue-skied June day in 1991, the sort of day one should *not* view a house, I suspect. Of course, we fell in love with the place. Who wouldn't, on a summer's day – a most unusual house at the end of a boreen that led to an inlet of Galway Bay. And yes, there were roses growing by the door. And the vendors were even throwing their four hens into the bargain, for God's sake! *The Good Life.* Things moved at a bewilderingly fast pace after that fateful day. Our own house went on the market. We put in a bid for Otterbrook (the Galway house). We waited and juggled and waited, trying to narrow the gap between what the sale of Sunset (in Greystones) would realise and our top offer for Otterbrook. We went for it and, by mid-July, the deal was done. The final piece of the jigsaw fell into place when Olive's sister Derry, who had been widowed two years earlier, moved to Bray in the same month of July. I now had a place to stay while working in Dublin.

Myself and Grennan, our Labrador dog, were the advance party when we moved house on 19th July 1991. The driver of the articulated removal van, having negotiated the boreen with great difficulty, got out, looked around and said with a sigh: 'Oh, it's a grand place alright – if you could stand the quiet!' A true Dub! And he was right. Killeenaran is a grand place, nestling on an inlet of Galway Bay, with the blue hills of Clare to the south and the mountains of Connemara beyond the lights of Galway city to the north. A magical place, full of wildlife and colour, and rich in heritage. Alongside our boreen alone, there is a sixth-century saint's penitential bed and a *cillín*, a children's graveyard.

For all its beauty, living here would mean a major adjustment in our lives. As I lay down to sleep on that first night, with Grennan at my side for company, I had niggling fears. Over the next twenty-four hours, the fears grew into panic. What had we done? What if this doesn't work? What if the whole thing was a mistake? I rang Olive. 'No,' she reassured me, 'we will be fine.' It was not a mistake. She had a good feeling about the place. Everything would be alright.

The reaction of family and work colleagues ranged from astonishment to admiration. Ye are mad! It cannot work! Well, fair play to ye! A lot of us dream it, but ye went and did it! We would obviously have a bit of convincing to do – of other people and, to be honest, of ourselves. There were major adjustments to be made. We had only one car. Olive would need it (we lived three miles from the nearest supermarket) and so, perforce, she began to drive. I would travel up and down by bus – not a prospect many would relish, but it did not bother me, initially. Declan went to boarding school at first. That did not work out, so he changed to a day school in Oranmore, eight miles away. Transport had to be arranged. A whole new pattern of living emerged, for all of us.

Olive took to country living immediately. She was a country girl for whom life had come full circle. She loved the natural beauty of the place, the relaxed pace of life and, above all, the people. She got to know the farmers who passed the door each day on their way to commonage. She would engage them in conversation and discuss the ills of the world and the parish. What they made of this glamorous woman coming to live in their midst can only be speculated on, but they warmed to her instantly. And why wouldn't they? Our circle of neighbours and friends grew, particularly with the help of Olive's parties. A memorable one in December 1991 celebrated my fiftieth birthday and the winning of another Japan Prize Radio Competition. Declan presented me with two Ailesbury ducks as a birthday present. Duck eggs for breakfast! Life was good!

10.45 a.m.,
Friday, 17th August 2001

My darling,
To the music of Dvorak's 'New World' Symphony ... where would I
be without music? It is such a balm. It evokes memories, yes, but it
links us in a special way. Thank God for Lyric FM. Had a long chat
with Anne O'Neill yesterday. You would (do!) like Anne. She's very
grounded, very perceptive. Warned me not to be crucifying myself
and told me to hold on to this beautiful love I have for you. Bet your
life!

This morning I read from Sr Stan's book, Now is the Time, *on*
death – prompted by Anne who recalled Stan telling me on air that
'Heaven is just a few inches above the tallest man.' Stan talks a lot
about 'letting go'. If we let go of painful experiences, we can be
transformed, we can grow. Letting go means living with the
greyness and foggy insecurity of life. We must trust this 'land of
don't know', because it is from here that wisdom comes forth. Living
with 'don't know' is letting go. It means waiting, accepting the not
knowing.

Yes, I accept that, but I need help to do so. Please help me, Lord.
Please help me, my love. 'Don't know,' according to Stan, is open to
miracles and insights. I need insights, love. Help me. Help me to
grow. What I'm not letting go is my beautiful love for you (our
beautiful love?). I love you so very, very much. This is my beautiful
unbidden mantra. So easy to say ... The dam burst. Such a comfort.

It's not clinging to the past. It's not trying to 'fix' the past. It's the
now – the beautiful now and the promise of the even more beautiful
future – an eternity. I'll wait, my darling. I'll accept the 'don't know'
but, in the meantime, I will love you so very, very much. 'All I Ask
of You' from The Phantom of the Opera *has become my theme*
song. I play it over and over.

No more talk of darkness
Forget those wide-eyed fears
I'm here, nothing can harm you
My words will warm and charm you

Let me be your freedom
Let daylight dry your tears
I'm here with you, beside you
To guard you and to guide you

Please let it be so, my darling.

John x

16

Parallel Tracks

Life was good – and creative – in the early-1990s. Before we moved west, I had begun writing fiction – something Olive had always encouraged. My first book, a children's novel entitled *The Summer of Lily and Esme,* was very well received, and won the Bisto Children's Book of the Year Award in 1992. Two more children's books followed before I launched into my magnum opus, an adult novel set in border country, covering a span of some sixty years. It was called *Generations of the Moon,* and it took me three years to write. It sold reasonably well, but I felt it should have done much better. I was, and am, very proud of it.

On the broadcasting front, *The Open Mind* began in 1989 and would run for thirteen years. It was a straightforward – mostly interview – programme, featuring interesting people and ideas, and it built up a committed audience over the years. I have been genuinely touched by the loyalty and affection of listeners. I will always remember the Cork woman who wrote, 'I never went past primary school, but you have been my third-level education.' I have always looked on myself as a conduit in bringing ideas to a wide audience, and have been privileged and fortunate to do so. I became involved in documentary-making – easily the most challenging and rewarding radio work – and made several educational and summer series. A series of important interviews, *My Education,* was published in book form in 1997 and, again, was very well received. Life was indeed good. Professional life.

On the home front, our relationship was becoming strained. As the Galway years went by, Olive and I seemed to be travelling on parallel tracks – but at least in the same direction. Olive was extremely happy in Galway, even though family and friends wondered how she could endure the winters, particularly, on her own for most of the week. For someone who was so outgoing and sociable, it was certainly a challenge, but she made her own life and was content. In my case, the weekend was too short. Five hours travelling in either direction shortened it even more, and my time in Otterbrook was largely taken up with the practicalities of life, such as maintaining the house and garden, helping with housework and preparing firewood for the week. We seemed to have less and less time together, although we managed a social life of sorts – a concert in Galway, meals out, parties, etc. It was an uneven time, however. The travelling was eventually getting to me, and four-hour bus trips became more a nightmare than a novelty. The lifestyle was eating into our relationship.

At the other end in Bray, Derry, Olive's sister, was becoming more and more dependent on me. She developed emphysema, and her health deteriorated quite rapidly from the mid-1990s onwards. I was stretched at both ends.

From the mid-1990s, Olive's health also became a serious problem. She began to suffer blackouts and developed blood-clotting problems. She was put on Warfarin tablets. Her speech became affected at times. She would know what she wanted to say, but sometimes 'the words would not come'. Equally, her writing gave indication that something was wrong. The writing itself became 'spidery' and she would have trouble with simple spelling and the order of words. Her personality seemed to change too. At times, she became irrational and unreasonable, the latter being something I would never have associated with her. I was genuinely worried for her. I pleaded with her to consider moving – at least to where she would be nearer the services she needed (we lived ten miles from her GP, pharmacy, etc.). What use could I be, 150 miles away, if she had a blackout and fell on the stone floor? She wouldn't hear of leaving Otterbrook. It was where she had found happiness. I had my job; she had Otterbrook. She agreed to get a panic alarm button, and she was surrounded by good neighbours. This was true but, in most cases, these were neighbours who had young families and their own busy lives to lead. Olive was adamant and, when Olive was adamant, that was the end of the argument. She was happy in Otterbrook. I knew that, but it was happiness at a price. With hindsight, I know I could and should have handled the situation better at times. I know I hurt her and was not always understanding of her plight, but the situation was growing more and more impractical. Derry's health deteriorated further. She became a prisoner in her apartment and, consequently, more and more dependent on me, to the extent that I had to spend some weekends in Bray.

9.55 a.m.,
Sunday, 19th August 2001

My darling, my darling, my darling,
I am so, so lost! Never imagined it could be as bad as this. I'm sure you're laughing now! Please don't. I'm hurting so much. Love you so much it hurts. It's beautiful but it hurts. Love you so very much. That's it. Nothing else matters. I need you so much. Need a sign that you're here.
    Watched Galway hurlers beat Kilkenny – they'll be dancing in Bernie's pub in Ballinderreen tonight! – and just cried my way through it. Not for Kilkenny – for you! And the evening was so long. Afraid of getting into a rut – you must help me. Be calm. Accept the not knowing … But Jesus, I love you so much – when the sunlight fell on that photo this evening, it was indescribable. The sheer radiance, the absolute beauty. How did I ever win you? Thank you, thank you, thank you, my one and only love. I couldn't look at you any longer – too, too much.
    Yesterday it rained – and rained – and rained! Went to Greystones to see Olga last night. As ever, she produced the champagne in your memory. She knows Loughnaphooey well and says it means Lake of the Winnowing Winds … Nice! She also reminded me that she had asked me in recent years if I still loved you and my reply was in the affirmative. Actually, what I said was 'Unfortunately, yes!' Sorry about the 'unfortunately'. I could never, would never, have left you. There was always that tie there. It was

called Love. Pity I didn't show it better but … All that is wiped out now. Has to be. I love you still, now, always and forever. Today I rang Gillian Deeny. She was a great help as ever. Reassured me that you loved me and were so proud of me.

So here I am. Drained. All cried out. Fondling your ring which is a great comfort. Longing for you. So lost. So lonely. Help me, pet. I must be patient. I must be calm. I love you so very, very, very much.

Guz x Guz x

A part of my reaction to all of this was to accept its inevitability, and plunge myself more and more into my work (I almost became a workaholic!). I would work late in the Radio Centre five nights a week. My programme output increased, but it was an unnatural and, ultimately, unhealthy lifestyle. The only real winners were RTÉ and the listeners who would enjoy my output. In 1999, I was diagnosed with having prostate cancer, and underwent a prostatectomy. Olive came up to Dublin while I was in hospital, and was so attentive and caring then, and subsequently during my convalescence in Galway. It proved, if proof were needed (and maybe it was) that, despite our problems, deep down there was a solid foundation to our relationship. It was proved again two years later, when Olive became seriously ill. It was a foundation of love. We argued, we differed, we lived in different worlds at times, but we loved each other, despite all. Life!

The 'Galway Experiment' worked for Olive, but, to be honest, it did not work for me. We had good times there, we made good friends, but the distance from work and the travelling ultimately put too much of a strain on our relationship. At the end of the day (literally), we all like to come *home* from work. Eventually Fate took a hand.

12.30 a.m.,
Tuesday, 21st August 2001

My darling,
Have just turned off a disgustingly violent film on television. Why I
watched it till then I don't know. That's one of the 2,379,643 reasons
I need you here …

Anyway, the big news! At 2.23 p.m. yesterday our little 'Lee-Lou'
gave birth to an 8lb baby girl. Everything went well – that's all the
detail I have. What could I do but cry – for you. Just by eight weeks
you missed it … I know you were there, but you know what I mean.
O my love, I hope she has some of your genes and much of your
beauty. It's a strange feeling being a granddad – I just want to share
it with you. I am so happy for Lisa and John, but, but, but … You,
my darling, you, you, you. Where are you, my pet? I hope John is
even a fraction as proud as I was when you gave birth to Lisa. I
remember I bought you an antique rocking chair! And when I first
visited you in Lourdes Hospital, you asked me, 'When can we have
another one?'

Bought a gold chain for your ring. The jeweller did say he could
split it and enlarge it to fit my finger, but no! I couldn't do that. So
now you nestle close to my heart – and it's a good feeling. Ray
Conniff is playing 'Dancing in the Dark' – how I wish it could be so,
my love. Love you, love you, love you. Someday we'll dance in the
light. Someday. Eight weeks. Eight long weeks. Clare says it will take
five years. What will take five years? For me to 'get over it'? I will
never rest until we meet again. Never.

But we have a grandchild. The line continues. And I'm glad it is
a girl. I knew a girl once. She was so beautiful that I married her.
Don't know what she saw in me, but I adored her. Still do. Still do.
Stay with me forever, my beautiful one. Forever young. Forever my
beautiful love.

John x

12.17 a.m.,
Wednesday, 22nd August 2001

My darling,
Today I heard our granddaughter cry on the phone. Such a wonderful feeling. It was very precious. Lisa's home! So proud of her 'too cute' baby. Part of her name will be Olivia ... Can't wait to see her.

Things to delight and remember. Read the inscription on Seamus Heaney's latest book.

In the everything flows and steady go of the world.

Lovely line. (It's about a perch!) In the everything flows and steady go of the world – I think of you, remember you, love you, adore you so. Another poem refers to Michael Collins – I remembered our visiting his birthplace last year. And it was good and warming.

Your ring close to my heart is such a comfort. I fondle it, kiss it, press it to my lips. Tonight Pat and Phelim Donlon had me in for a meal and a chat, a listen to Phelim's jazz collection, a cigar and a cognac. Pat is a wonderful friend. When I asked Phelim if he would play the piano for me, he played 'Moonlight Sonata' and 'Send in the Clowns'. Were you turning the pages or what? It drew me closer and closer to you.

So, my love, in the everything flows and steady go of the world, I am – like the perch – 'on hold' with you, for you, through you. The dam has burst and my God! – is the seed in my heart blossoming??

And now there's little Olivia. Fruit of the fruit of our love. Hope she looks like you, is you. What a start in life that would be? Your photo rests on my lap. Your ring rests on my lips. Peace. Love. You. You. You. Nothing else matters. Olive. All love. My precious one.

All my love,
John x

17

The End of the Adventure

At the end of April 2001, Olive and I returned to Otterbrook. It was an emotional homecoming for Olive. Nine months previously, she had left home to go up to Dublin for routine tests which would take no more than a couple of days. On her second day in hospital, she suffered severe haemorrhaging and ended up having a hysterectomy – a more than serious operation in her case, given her respiratory problems. That was only the beginning of the nightmare. Five weeks in hospital and a nursing home, and then back to Bray to convalesce. Her sister, Derry, broke her shoulder in a fall, and had to be hospitalised for an operation. Olive and I looked after her. The plan was that we would be home in Galway for Christmas.

Two weeks before Christmas, Olive fell down the stairs in Derry's apartment and broke her neck. She spent Christmas, and the next three months, in hospital, her head encased in that awful 'halo'. To complicate matters, she lost her swallow in the trauma of the fall, and had to be fed by tube directly into her stomach. The medical team were also concerned about her balance when she began to walk again. It was a bleak scenario, but Olive Quinn was always a fighter. Slowly, she edged her way back, recovering her swallow with the aid of a wonderful young speech therapist, and finally shedding the 'halo' in March. Three further weeks in a nursing home and finally back to Bray. Four days later, her beloved sister Derry succumbed quite suddenly to the emphysema. Trauma upon trauma. When Olive was strong enough, I took a month's leave from work, and took her back to Otterbrook.

Otterbrook,
12.15 a.m.,
Saturday, 25th August 2001

My darling,
Christ, it's hard coming back here with no you. I bawled for the first thirty minutes. Everything here is you – furniture, new floors, paintings, silver, china. What will I do with all this stuff? More to the point, what will I do without you? Miss you so much – especially here. Couldn't hack it at all at first. Went out and cut the grass and then wrote a poem about your presence here. Calmer now. I suppose it is your presence. I said to you earlier that if I didn't feel you, sense you, hear you, I would just fall apart. I really feel I would ...

Played the little snatch of cassette tape from the Navan days when the children were small. It was so lovely to hear your voice – even your little 'Hmmms' – although it made me desperately lonely.

I need you all about me, all the time, always loving me – is that being greedy? Just a measure of how much I love you. Visited your grave on the way down here. I know you're not there – it's just a point of contact – but it only magnified my love and my loss. Rang Lisa tonight. Eva Olivia has settled a bit more and is just 'too cute'. Can't wait to see her, but I know I'll fall to pieces when I do – because I'll be thinking of you and loving you, which I do with all the intensity, tenderness and depth which I can muster. With all my soul, I give myself to you, my beautiful one, my only one.

John x

As I mowed the lawn at sunset
Did I see you
Give a little wave
On returning from your walk?

Did I see you
Move about the kitchen
Making your 'tup of tea'?
Did I watch you
Watch the sun set
From your conservatory chair?

Did I smile
As you gesticulated
To a friend on the phone?

Did I notice you
Glide past the window
With a little glass
Of Muscadet?

And when the dark descended
And I came in
Exhausted
Did I hear you call out
'If you're making
A tup of tea
I wouldn't mind another' …?

Of course I did –
But when I went to make it,
The dark was all around …

May is my favourite month of the year, and it was good to be in Otterbrook for that month. It was a special time for us. We were closer than we had been for a long time, moving at our own pace, enjoying freedom and quiet. Olive built up her strength with daily walks and nightly glasses of Guinness. We lived royally on the wine and champagne I had stocked up for the Christmas we never had. We went out for meals. We were at ease with each other and with life. It was a special time, cherished all the more in retrospect. It was meant to be.

By the time I returned to work in June, Olive had recovered sufficiently to lead an independent life again. She was able to drive the car, do her shopping, enjoy the peace of her beloved Otterbrook. On her birthday, 16th June, I wrote on her card, 'To Molly Bloom, Love and Happiness, Miracle Girl!' Truly, she was a miracle girl. There was no one like her. Mindful of how we had 'postponed' Christmas, I booked us into Kelly's Hotel in Rosslare for a week later in the month. When I told her, she was like a child at Christmas. 'Don't tell anyone where we're going,' she said excitedly.

'Why not?' I asked.

'I just want it to be our secret.'

It was just like old times.

12.50 a.m.,
Sunday, 25th August 2001

My darling,
Just back from Henehan's barbecue. Very pleasant – loads of food and drink – but my heart wasn't really in it (guess where it was!). I was anxious to leave, when Ann McDonagh arrived and what happened was so wonderful. She is so perceptive ...

'Olive for me was ethereal. She was not for this planet at all, not tuned in to our wavelength. She was just passing through and is now where she needs to be ... an angel without wings ... my image is of her wearing long flowing clothes ... gliding through a crowded room ... the hair perfect, the fine chiselled features ... she is on a different level now ... very content and very close to you ...'

It was so wonderful, so real. I told her what I had been though. She understands the 'damburst', what Lois (whom she knows) remembers. So comforting, so reassuring. I am so indebted to her and told her so repeatedly. Her reply?

'There is no such thing as coincidence. Everything is meant to happen at a particular time. I wasn't going to come here tonight, but I changed my mind. When I did come, I didn't know you would be here. It was meant to be.'

O my ethereal one, I am so happy about that. No one but Ann had that perception of you. She is especially gifted. Where does that leave you? This reminds me of meeting your angel in Stephen's Green … As I said to Ann, wasn't I lucky? Yes – and no! Luck had absolutely nothing to do with it. It was meant to be! I am so uplifted. Thank you, Ann, for such insight.

'And there will be further insights, little ways forward, revealing more and more to you. Hold on to that beautiful love.'

Thank you, my beautiful ethereal one. I was so low going down to Henehan's. Ann transformed me. You organised it. I know that. As Marie Barrett said, nothing will be a problem any more. I love you, my precious one. It was meant to be. Deo Gratias.

All my love – always,
John x

1.45 a.m.,
Thursday, 30th August 2001

My darling,
Poetry rules this day. I was given a wonderful poem – 'Watercolour for a Widower' – by Aidan Mathews. I was so deeply touched. It demands several readings but it's a wonderful sea-poem, echoing my own feelings: 'sea of love, sea of loss'.

> This, the last birth and the most bitter,
> Will taste of salt wind and sand dunes forever …

But it is balanced by the coming of our granddaughter –

> an olive branch
> Washes in on a warm wave
> From a saltwater uterus ...

Exquisite! As Aidan predicted, my eyes

> fill up and fulfil
> With something strange and saline ...

How often have they filled up, my love, and have burned and stung ...
*   Then I bought Douglas Dunn's* Elegies *(as recommended by John*
O'Donohue). In one poem, he 'sieves through' twenty years with his
beloved until he reaches,

> The truth that waits for me with its loud grief.

I too sieve – through thirty-five years of presence, to help me cope
with absence. Next I came across a little book of Joan Walsh
Anglund's poems that I gave you in 1968. I had especially marked
for you the lines:

> Just beyond my wisdom are words
> Which would explain everything ...

Is that uncanny or ... or is it just another one of those little steps that
Ann McDonagh mentioned? Probably! Beyond understanding, beyond
wisdom – indeed. I must be patient. Wait. Accept the 'not knowing'.

Help me, my darling,
John x

WATERCOLOUR FOR A WIDOWER

for John

Your wife floats out to sea and is lost
In a real swimsuit, in actual surf.
This, the last birth and the most bitter,
Will taste of salt wind and sand dunes forever
With the medical stench of the ocean's ointment.
Shorelines, outlines, waterlines:
The wet mess they once called the margin.
You stand with your two feet on the ground,
Your toes bedded in hard strand
Like a climber's slowly slipping grip …
Even Sherpa Tenzing and Hillary
In their face-masks and oxygen tanks
Traced at the holy pinnacle
The fossils of starfish in the snow clouds
To go with a jetty twenty miles inland.

Now a grand-daughter, an olive branch,
Washes in on a warm wave
From a saltwater uterus
Among girls in white hospital gowns,
Angels with steel oxygen cylinders.

You are the shell of the man you once were.
Put your ear to its aperture.
Listen to the salt that it came from:
Sea of love, sea of loss,
The Aral Sea, the Red Sea, the Sea of Atlantis.

As they lift the child and lower her in,
Her fontanel streaming like Mesopotamia,
Will it be any wonder at all,
Salt-of-the-earth man, gilly of the middle-ground,
That even your eyes fill up and fulfil

With something strange and saline –
Like the Tupperware flask of sea-water
I brought home with me from the Mediterranean
And kept on my desk like a skull for a year
Before giving it back to the basin?
(Aidan Mathews)

London,
10.50 p.m.,
Tuesday, 11th September 2001

My darling,
Here I am – and your granddaughter is gorgeous! Too cute, as Lisa would say. I think (hope) she has your eyes. Lisa says she definitely can arch her eyebrows like you did when you were cross.

But, just as I walked into Lisa's apartment, an awful atrocity was unfolding in New York and Washington ... Seemed like Armageddon. I can't really talk about it. All I know is I'm glad you're out of such a world. It really would be too much for you, too distressing. I recall writing to you when Robert Kennedy was assassinated – we were of one mind, but couldn't speak. So I'm glad you are safe and removed from all of this – even if it means you are removed from me. Holding Eva Olivia was bittersweet – how you would dote over her! Can't get those poor people in the Twin Towers out of my mind. Can't get you out of my mind. Would I want to? A black, black day in world history. Hold me. Together we will triumph. We are one.

We two alone will sing like birds i' th' cage ...

I love you so very much. That conquers even the blackest day. Thank you, my beautiful one.

John x

Victoria Station,
2.10 p.m.,
Friday, 14th September 2001

My darling,
Just back from an amazing trip to Selsey to interview Sir Patrick Moore. What a crazy evening! We had a family of four visitors as 'audience' for most of the interview! The interview was done in bits and pieces but it was wonderful. Patrick is a loveable rogue who lost his loved one to Hitler sixty years ago. It still hurts, so he knows how I feel. Then the neighbours arrived, especially the 'mad Irishwoman' (Patrick's words) Eileen Nolan. And the whiskey flowed – and I had no lunch … Eileen reaffirmed your presence – 'she is here now, glorying in all of this'. I know you would enjoy the fun … too much for me! Patrick prepared a lovely dinner and insisted I stay the night. By the time we reached the coffee, I was fading fast, had to excuse myself and retire to bed. Gone in ten seconds! You were probably mortified but – admit it – you would probably have been the same yourself!

Dreamt of you briefly. I threw a book towards you in disgust over something, but apologised later when I took you in my arms and said, 'I love you so very much.' Nice! Patrick had a lovely breakfast ready for me. He is the perfect host. I went for a walk on Selsey Beach where I wrote a poem to you.

Today is a World Day of Mourning for America's lost ones. At 11 a.m. I stood by Patrick's observatory and thought of them – and you – and how infinitesimal this planet is in the scheme of things. And how much hatred and futility there is on it. Like I said, you are well off out of it – only I still miss you like crazy.

John x

On Selsey Beach
I think of you
As I listen to
The symphony of the sea.

On Selsey Beach
I pray for you
And that we two
Will share eternity.

On Selsey Beach
I long for you
To walk with me
Along the pebbled shore.

On Selsey Beach
I call to you
And sing my love
To the ocean's echoing roar.

12.20 p.m.,
Tuesday, 18th September 2001

My darling, my beautiful bride of thirty-three years, my love,
This is the day. This is the day you made me so proud and happy.
This is the day I slipped the ring on your finger and promised to
love, honour and obey, in sickness and in health, till death do us
part. And now it has – and that ring nestles close to my heart. Made
a bags of that promise at times, but we stuck at it. All that 'stuff'
that got in the way is gone now. I can see clearly now. You are in
perpetual light and wisdom. You know now.
I can see clearly that all I ever wanted was your happiness. That's
all. Ever. Ever. Ever. I was so young and innocent then but I know
one thing. You were for me and I was for you. That's why our
wedding day was so wonderful. I never enjoyed a wedding like it.
You were so, so beautiful. When I reflect now that you did all the
organising yourself – you who had been at death's door two years

earlier – you were brilliant. So beautiful, so radiant, so poised, so calm. Thank you for the memories. I was not worthy. Truly I wasn't.

Such wonderful memories. Your late arrival (car wouldn't start!), walking down the aisle, the reception, my singing 'Try to Remember', escaping to Blessington, your missing cosmetics bag (Temper! Temper!), our first gentle night together. Try to remember indeed. I don't have to, my precious one. It's all there. And as the song says, I will follow.

7 p.m., Galileo's Restaurant
Nice meal. Brandy and soda in our honour. Looking through the album, especially at the wedding photo. To be honest, I can't look at it. You're just – ethereal. Christ, what was I doing there at all? I was so honoured that you chose to commit your life to me. I was as indescribably happy then as I am indescribably lonely now.

I live only for the day when we can be together again – forever, with no 'stuff' in the way. If that's not feasible, there's no point. I might just as well crumble to pieces here in London town. I have never felt the depth of emotion I feel now. It is pure love – absolutely pure – exhilarating and heart-breaking at the same time. Thirty-three years ago this evening I held you in my arms and everything in this world was perfect. Now you are beyond this world and I wait – impatiently – but I wait. How wonderful it will be.

Later still!
Just home from The Phantom of the Opera. Wonderful production. Of course I cried all the way through 'our song' – 'All I Ask of You' – but it was a good way to celebrate our anniversary. Didn't we have a good time? The seed in my heart continues to blossom – wonderfully, beautifully.

All my love, always,
John x

Epilogue

When I go back to Otterbrook now, I make straight for the black leather coat [not the original one of course!] *that hangs on the hook just inside the door. I caress its soft material, inhale your scent that still clings to its sleeves, and say, 'Here I am, Eddie Duchins.' The tears flow.*

Here I am indeed, and where are you? The great mystery. 'There,' I hope, happy, blissfully eternally happy [all I ever wanted for you was to be happy, remember?] *but 'here' too. I believe in your presence – totally. That's why I talk to you all the time.* [Yeh! Yeh! I know – much more than I ever did when you were alive.] *That's why I write constantly to you – not that you need my letters now. You know it all now. You are in the light. It's me that needs the letters. I need, desperately, to be in touch with you. I need your presence. That's why I recognised you in St Stephen's Green when the down-and-out whispered in my ear, 'The seed in your heart shall blossom.' You and he were right, of course. The seed of love has blossomed wonderfully, beautifully, in my heart – and it continues to blossom. Thank you, my darling. It's the strangest mixture of feelings. I am at once heartbroken by your absence and totally consumed by your 'presence' – more in love with you than I ever thought possible.*

Is it so with you? Please love me. I know you give me little signs now and then and I know I must be patient. That's the hardest part. A wise man said long ago 'Amor est Passio' *('Love is Suffering') and he was right!*

It's a hard and lonely road without you, and while family and friends have been supportive (especially wonderful friends I have made since you died), ultimately it's a road I must walk alone. I miss you – even to argue with! I miss you, terribly, frighteningly. And I need you, now more than ever. So please stay close to me – as close as your wedding ring which I now wear on a chain around my neck – or else I fall apart.

Love you. Miss you. Above all, above all, thank you. Thank you for walking into my life thirty-six years ago – and staying in it, especially when, occasionally, you must have been tempted to walk out of it! We had our highs and our lows but, in the general mystery of life, we did alright, Eddie Duchins. We did more than alright. Don't know about you, but I'd do it all again!

Of all the throat-swab joints in all the world, you had to walk into mine, swish that black leather coat and flash that smile …

Deo Gratias

John

And it was lovely then
And you were lovely then
And we were young
And so in love
And it was lovely then

– And will be so again
And will be so again …

II. SEED OF LOVE, SEED OF LIFE

Introduction

A LITTLE EXERCISE IN SELF-INTERROGATION

So you want to write again. Haven't you done it all – told all about yourself and Olive? End of story?

No. Not at all. The story continues. Love grows. Loss is permanent. Life goes on. How do you cope with them – love, loss, life? That's an ongoing story.

Worth telling?

I think so. A lot of people enjoyed the original story. Said they found it honest. It struck chords with them. I was very moved by their reactions.

Some examples?

I could fill another book with reactions alone, but here's a selection:

> I found your book touching and inspiring.
> *(Cardinal Cahal Daly)*

> I was gripped and moved by your book from beginning to end. It is about the best kind of giving – thanksgiving. A grammar of gratitude for Olive. *(Mary Redmond, Irish Hospice Movement)*

> We found your book a great solace after the death of our beautiful son, Sean. *(Una O'Hagan and Colm Keane)*

I read the entire book in two and a half hours and cried at its honesty and raw emotion. Your book will, I feel, change my life. *(Evelyn Ward)*

It is a superb tribute to love and marriage. It restores one's faith. *(Muriel McCarthy)*

I found the letters really amazing. I would say that the love you and Olive share is mystical. *(Dolores Grady)*

You achieve that delicate balance of making a memoir both personal and universal. It reads like a film and I'm still upset after watching it. *(Roger McGough)*

I had heard your radio programme but the book fleshed out the epiphany in a surprisingly fresh way. My teacher in Chicago – Mircea Eliade – used to speak of 'kratophany' for such a manifestation of the sacred power of disclosure. *(Sean Dwan)*

It moved me to the core of my being. I know I will keep it and re-read it from time to time, because it ignited so many different emotions in me. *(Sr Stanislaus Kennedy)*

I could not leave your book down. I was riveted by the love story with the frank ups and downs that all of us experience in our marriages. *(Joan Wilson)*

So why now?

It's a decade on from Olive's death in 2001. And at the end of 2011 I will be seventy years of age. Seven decades. A milestone at which to reflect.

Have you thought of a title for this part of the story?

Originally, I didn't see the need for a separate title, but my friend Regina suggested *Seed of Love, Seed of Life*, which I like. She was thinking of what the down-and-out said to me in St Stephen's Green – 'The seed in your heart shall blossom'. It was so startling at the time, so intriguing, so poetic – and ultimately so prophetic. The seed of love has blossomed so wonderfully and continues to do so. In doing so it has revealed to me a whole new perspective on life.

So how will you tell the story?

Well, the letters to Olive will be a big part of it. Ten years on, I still write to her. And the poems – they are just another form of conversation. They are by no means literary gems, but little messages that occur to me and which I find easy to jot down impromptu on the back of an envelope or on a napkin in a cafe or on the train. Spur of the moment stuff, but important to me. And there's also the 'Book of Consolations'.

Do explain!

It's simply a journal given to me by a friend, in which I record words that impress and console me, regarding love and loss – a verse of a poem, lines from a song, an excerpt from a book or newspaper article, a letter. Over the years it has built up into a rich anthology of consolations.

I have to ask you this question. Is there not a danger that an enterprise like this could be seen as a kind of ego-trip?

It's a fair question. I would hate that it be interpreted as such. I am not that kind of person. It's a trip alright – a journey of extraordinary blessing for which I feel totally unworthy. I just want to share that journey with others. No more than that.

And how will you tell that story?

Initially, I thought I would tell it chronologically, but then I felt a straight narrative might not encompass all of the issues and influences I would hope to include – so instead, I will build the story around themes such as Memory, Regret, Gratitude, Love, Milestones, Time, etc. I hope it works.

Good luck with it so!

Thanks. Stick around. I'll need your help!

The Angel of St Stephen's Green

Although I have written about the St Stephen's Green encounter in Part One, I feel I must return to it here, as over the years its significance in my life has deepened considerably.

I sat on a bench in the Green, still raw and grieving six weeks after my wife's death. I paused there, conscious of the association of place with memory. We had sat there on a beautiful autumn evening less than a year before. No need for words. Just being there together. And now here I was, leafing through my photo album, when this down-and-out approaches. A chance encounter? Maybe. Maybe not.

I could easily have dismissed him with a cigar and walked off, but I stayed to hear his story. It's what Olive would have done. She would have been totally concerned for him, ensuring he had a bed for the night in a hostel, trying to help him get his life back on an even keel. The Patron of Lost Causes. So I listened to his story. A heartbreaking tale of wrong decisions taken. There but for the grace of God go any of us. He was so engaging and witty, breaking off from his story to pass comment on the deadly serious joggers consulting their stopwatches as they passed. He knew nothing about me. All the conversation had been about his life – until I rose to go and told him I had lost my wife six weeks previously. And then, that extraordinary gesture.

He embraced me and whispered in my ear – 'The seed in your heart shall blossom.'

Here we had been, talking of horse-racing, cheating, alcoholism, marriage break-up, homelessness … and now he comes out with this beautifully poetic statement. 'The seed in your heart shall blossom.' As I walked away in a somewhat confused state, I turned to wave a final goodbye. My friend had rejoined his mates. He mimed his parting words back to me – thumb and finger pressed together ('the seed'), pointing to the heart, and then a great circle described with both arms. I walked on and he was gone out of my life. A chance encounter? Maybe not.

As the letter written that evening indicates, I had worked out this encounter before I got back to RTÉ. That was no 'wino'. That was Olive, surely. That was her way of saying, 'You'll be alright. I'm here. I'll look after you.' I remember thinking with a wry smile, that is typical of Olive's sense of humour. Why not have a tall, fragrant, willowy blonde wrap her arms around me and tell me the seed in my heart would blossom? Why had it to be a dishevelled, smelly 'wino'? I could hear Olive giggling in the background.

It was a surreal encounter, and as I told people about it, their reaction was the same. You were blessed, they said. You were specially chosen. When I told the late John O'Donohue, his reaction was immediate. 'That was an angel. No question about it. The word "angelus" literally means a messenger. He was sent to you with a message of hope and consolation.'

His words reinforced my own initial feelings on that August evening in 2001.

And so the down-and-out (I had never established his actual name) became the Angel of St Stephen's Green to me. His poetic words became a mantra to me, particularly on 'down' days. And they were borne out with the passing days and months and years. The seed of love did blossom in my heart in the most wonderful way. I fell in love with Olive McKeever all over again and that love has continued to deepen and blossom outrageously in the purest and most complete sense. The most beautiful love, surpassing that of 'the first time around'. Yes, I am specially chosen. Yes, I am blessed. *Deo et Oliviae Gratias.*

And what of the Angel? A few times since the encounter I strolled and sat in the Green, wishfully hoping but knowing in my heart that we would not meet again. One meeting was enough. The seed was blossoming, but I had not heard the last of the Angel yet. His story would have a sad ending. In January 2005 I got a phone call from a friend in Dublin who had been told by Alice Leahy of TRUST (a charity that cares for the homeless) that the Angel had been found dead in a Dublin hostel, probably from a drug overdose. Alice had come across him in her work with TRUST and recognised him as 'the Angel' when she read *Sea of Love, Sea of Loss*. His name (or at least one of his names) was Michael Kelly.

I cried when I heard the news. I had only known Michael for fifteen minutes but he had played a huge role in my life at the most fragile time of my life. I would cry even more for Michael a few weeks later when I learned that despite the best efforts of Alice, An Garda Síochána and Interpol, no trace of Michael's family could be found. I found that very hard to take. Yes, he may have broken hearts or ruined lives, but he was a person, a human being who deserved to be reclaimed by his own and given a decent burial. He would have ended up in a pauper's grave had Alice not organised his funeral and had him buried in a special TRUST plot in Glasnevin cemetery.

At the midnight hour on the eve of his burial in February 2005 I wrote these lines:

FOR MICHAEL

You came to me in the summer
When my heart was broken and low
You came to me in the summer
And gave me the gift of hope
   And nobody came to claim him
   And nobody wanted to know
   The Angel of St Stephen's Green
   Was cast aside by his own

You came to me in the summer
When each day was darkest night
You came to me in the summer
And gave me the gift of light

And nobody came to claim him
And nobody wanted to know
The Angel of St Stephen's Green
Was cast aside by his own

You came to me in the summer
When no birds sang above
You came to me in the summer
And gave me the gift of love
  And nobody came to claim him
  And nobody wanted to know
  The Angel of St Stephen's Green
  Was cast aside by his own

'The seed in your heart shall blossom'
You whispered in my ear
The seed in YOUR heart now blossoms
As harvest-time draws near.

I say a prayer for Michael – and all the Michael Kellys in this world – every night. It's the least I can do in gratitude for a fifteen-minute encounter that raised me up at a dark time and has continued to bear me aloft ever since.

But the story still does not end there. In the same year – 2005 – I received a letter from Peter Hannan, a noted Jesuit theologian and writer. He was writing a book on the meaning and beauty of the Mass, and wished to know if he could draw on *Sea of Love, Sea of Loss* for part of it. I was completely flattered – and puzzled. What could my story have to contribute to a book on the meaning and beauty of the Mass?

Peter took as the title for his book *Love Remembered*, from the lines of a Shakespearean sonnet:

For thy sweet love remembered such wealth brings
That then I scorn to change my state with kings.

(Those lines from Sonnet 29 accurately sum up my own feelings).

He uses films such as *Babette's Feast* and *Lantana* to illustrate the meaning of the Mass, and in one whole section – 'Immersing Ourselves in the Love We Remember' – he draws parallels from *Sea of Love, Sea of Loss*. Five years on, I am still overwhelmed by this. How could the story of a relationship – a relatively simple story – achieve this status? Peter Hannan argues that immersion in personal loss sensitises us and makes us more compassionate to others who have suffered loss. In the St Stephen's Green incident, it was only after experiencing my own loss that I could 'so graciously be with someone who has lost his good name and his livelihood'.

I agree with Peter. Loss has sensitised me to the plight of others. The Angel of St Stephen's Green is but one example. The seed in my heart has blossomed wonderfully and continues to blossom. Those prophetic words brought Olive present to me in a new way. Peter Hannan sees a parallel between that new presence and the new and mysterious way Jesus became present to his disciples after his death. On the road to Emmaus, the disciples – overcome by loss – did not immediately recognise their master. It was only when they listened to him that they realised who he was and 'their hearts burned for him'. I am totally humbled that a reader of my story could draw such a parallel, but certainly, on my way back to RTÉ that wonderful August evening, I knew I had met Olive in a new way and my heart burned for her – fiercely. A 'chance' decision to pause in the Green and a 'chance' encounter there had changed my life.

Time

Kelly's Hotel, Rosslare,
1.16 p.m.,
25th June 2009

> Anniversary day again
> Eight years –
> Is it really?
> I would have said four,
> Maybe five –
> Believe me, it's eight!
> The longer, the closer …
> You, stretched in the sun-chair
> Happy, smiling.
> Would you like a Tio Pepe
> Before lunch?

Sure you'll be grand. Eight years. Isn't time the great healer? That's what they say. Is it the great healer? I think not and I am not alone. Joan Wilson agrees with me. Joan lost her daughter Marie in the Enniskillen bombing, her son Peter in a road accident and her wonderful husband Gordon from a heart attack. All in the space of eight years. Joan knows more about loss and grief than most of us. She wrote a bereavement memoir in 2001 – *All Shall Be Well: A Bereavement Anthology and Companion* – and one chapter of that book is entitled 'Time Does Not Heal'. The loss of a loved one is a wound and …

… these wounds never heal completely. Your life will not be the same as it was and once you let this really sink in, it will be an important milestone in your healing process … Time teaches you how to cope – provided you are willing to be taught and to move on.

Yes, you learn to cope and accommodate, but the wound remains – no matter how much time passes, be it one day or one thousand and one days.

Kelly's Hotel, Rosslare,
22nd March 2004
(1001 days later …)

1001

1001 nights
1001 days too
1001 reasons
For missing you

1001 longings
1001 dreams
1001 whys
And no answers, it seems

1001 memories
1001 tears
1001 smiles
Down all the years

1001 wishes
Of happiness for you
1001 wishes
That I'll share it too

10.20 p.m.,
Tuesday, 29th May 2003

My darling,
Only today I discovered that yesterday marked 100 weeks. One
hundred weeks … I know it means literally nothing to you. How
wonderful for you. Incomprehensible for us. But 100 weeks – more
like 100 years. Long, long weeks. Long, long time. A lot of downs,
some wonderful ups. Miss you terribly, still. Please don't laugh or
say I told you so! I really, really, really miss you so much. Some very
lonely moments. Easy to fall into a rut. Please lift me, hold me.

And yet amid the loneliness, I feel so close to you. How
wonderful it will be … As someone said – 'If only we could realise
eternity.' For now I'm not sure if I want to stay here in Otterbrook.
Feel isolated at times. The book is for me a treasure. I've sent so
many copies to so many people – so that they will know about you!
In most cases, not even an acknowledgement. Why are people like
that? Me is very lonely. Please help. Please, please, please.

John x

P.S. I've just had a most helpful chat with Brenda Sweeney. She
really is so good to me and for me. The Angel of Ballinamore –
where she says the book is the talk of the town. Thank you! I do love
you so much.

The wound that is loss can be reopened by the most trivial thing
– a piece of music, a souvenir trinket. Even by happening across
the bill for our 1968 honeymoon …

12.30 a.m.,
12th July 2003

THE HONEYMOON BILL

Do you realise
That I spent
Fifty Pounds Seven and Six
I'll repeat that –
Fifty Pounds Seven and Six
On our honeymoon?
You want proof?
There's the bill –
Casey's Hotel, Glengarriff
Room Five
    (AHHH – ROOM FIVE!)
19th September 1968
One pot of tea – two shillings
    (WHAT THE HELL – IT WAS OUR HONEYMOON!)
19th–26th September
1 week @ £20 each
Total – *Forty Pounds!*
    (HE THREW IT AROUND LIKE CONFETTI …)
26th–27th September
1 day @ 57/6 each
Five Pounds Fifteen
    (THE BOUNDER – AN EXTRA DAY!)
27th–28th September
Apartments (?) and breakfast
Three Pounds Ten
    (IS THERE NO END …?)
Ten per cent service charge
Four Pounds Eighteen and Six
    (HALF A WEEK'S SALARY …)
Less deposit – *Five Pounds*

And 28th September
– All right, let's go for it! –
Two luncheons
at ten shillings each
Plus service charge
    (OF COURSE)
Two shillings
Making a grand total of
Fifty Pounds Seven and Six
Was I reckless or what?
Weren't you lucky
You married a filthy rich teacher?
Wasn't I lucky?
Boy – wasn't I lucky?
And rich too
Beyond compare
Far beyond
Fifty Pounds Seven and Six
Thank you.

Casey's Hotel,
Glengarriff, Co. Cork,
11.53 p.m.,
Sunday, 18th September 2005

My darling,
Recognise the date? Recognise the address? (Too well, she said. Too well!) Yes, I've come back, thirty-seven years later. Happy Anniversary! Casey's has changed a lot. Recently refurbished. A night here now will cost me more than eight days then! But the memories flood back. A totally beautiful bride, total happiness and almost total disbelief that she should have chosen ME – shy, reclusive, inexperienced, introverted ME – but she did and for that I loved and adored her then, now, and will do forever more. That's no sentimental, nostalgic bullshit. That's how I feel. It's how YOU feel that worries me – especially when I have these occasional weird dreams … But it was lovely then and you were lovely then … I

remember the lovely drives around West Cork, the mother and son from Britain who played Scrabble endlessly ('Oh, mother – you are an absolute TOAD!'), the beginning of a long voyage of discovery ... There can be only one word here in this little room thirty-seven years later – THANKS – for you, for what you stood for, for three beautiful children, for the memories. I know there are unhappy memories, but THANK you.

On our wedding day I sang to you –

> Try to remember the kind of September
> When you were a tender and callow fellow ...
> Deep in December, it's nice to remember
> The fire of September that made us mellow ...

Deep in this December of our marriage, I remember and I follow, and I thank you. Maybe one night here is enough. I have come back and remembered and that is enough. A verse in the hotel brochure says of Glengarriff –

> When once you've heard her laughter gay
> You weep when you are torn away.
> A thousand memories call you back
> For one more day ...

It could equally apply to the beautiful woman I brought here as my bride thirty-seven years ago today.

Love you more than ever.
John x

4.45 p.m.,
Tuesday, 23rd May 2006

IN SAILS CAFE, GALWAY

The world goes by.
A child has new runners
And proudly wears
One of them
And one old one.
An American
With rain-hat
And walking-stick
Tells his companion
He just doesn't understand …
A girl is texting …
The world goes by.
Me? I've just had
Tea for one
And a muffin …
It's not easy
Sailing alone.

Memory

In his *Letter of Consolation,* written to his father on the death of his mother, Henri Nouwen further emphasises that real grief is not healed by time ...

> If time does anything, it deepens our grief. The longer we live, the more fully we become aware of who she was for us, and the more intimately we experience what her love meant for us. Real deep love is, as you know, very unobtrusive, seemingly easy and obvious, and so present that we take it for granted. Therefore, it is often only in retrospect – or better, in memory – that we fully realise its power and depth ...

Its power and its depth ... Forty years after that fateful walk around the Boiler House lawn in Blanchardstown, the power and the depth of the love that was born that day (see p. 43) resonated within me. On that evening the line from Virgil – *haec olim meminisse iuvabit* (one day it will delight us to remember these things) – came to mind.

7.13 p.m.,
Tuesday, 30th May 2006

My darling, darling,
This is IT! The Holy Hour! Laugh you may, but this hour forty years ago was the most wonderful hour of my life till then – and it is sacred to me now and will be forever more. This is the hour that changed my life, MADE my life. The Boiler House Walk in Blanchardstown, 1966.

The wonderful 'lost in the woods' escapade, followed by those sixteen laps of the Boiler House lawn. The laughter (whose, I wonder!). The thrill of just being with you and talking with you – privately – learning about our families, our interests, our lives. Reading the diary brings it all back.

I was so green, so naive. Never had a real date in twenty-four years and this was my first! Thank you, thank you, thank you. You'll never know what that day meant to me. Haec olim meminisse iuvabit – indeed! It was actually our second walk of the day. Earlier we went 'up to the prison fence for inspiration after Mass …' How blessed and smitten I was – 'she is so charming and unpretentious … her care for the children (etc.) … She's for me'! She was indeed and is and will be forever more.

I know you 'didn't want to get involved …' When you started writing you never realised you would one day meet me. I thought you were 'too wonderful for me'. BUT you must see now that it was all MEANT TO BE. Maybe, years later, you regretted ever making that walk, 'getting involved …' Maybe not. I pray not. No point in speculating on that now. For now, for that wonderful, sacred hour forty years ago, I am so thankful. I thank you and bless you forever, my beautiful one, whom I didn't deserve and should have loved so much more. I just couldn't believe my luck. All my dreams, all my fantasies, realised in that sacred hour. It had to be you. I am totally convinced of that.

There was only one thing on my mind then (No! Not THAT!) and there is only one thing on my mind now – YOU. Stunningly beautiful, glorious, wonderful you. Of course, we had awful days in later life, but we're only human. This day forty years ago was the DAY OF DAYS, the day I really got to know you, the day I fell totally in love with you. Deo Gratias. I love you now even more than then. IS THAT CLEAR TO YOU? You consume my days and I would have it no other way. Please, please, please talk to me – in whatever way – and say all I want to hear – that it is equally so with you. That is all that matters to me, Olive McKeever. All. All. All. IS THAT CLEAR?

Haec olim meminisse iuvabit doesn't even begin to sum it up. I walked on air. I was a different person, all because of you. Thank

*you. Love you to absolute bits. Need your love and presence so
desperately. Please know that and talk to me.*

John x

In his book *Anam Chara*, John O'Donohue also wrote beautifully
about memory: 'Memory is one of the most beautiful realities of the
soul ... It is the place where our vanished days secretly gather ...'
 He continued his theme in *Eternal Echoes*:

> The kingdom of memory is full of the ruins of presence. It
> is astonishing how faithful experience actually is: how it
> never vanishes completely ... Nothing is ever lost or
> forgotten! It is only through the act of remembrance,
> literally re-membering, that we can come to poise, integrity
> and courage.

It is not a case of trying to hold on to the past in a nostalgic way.
Rather is it a way of maintaining the presence of a loved one whose
absence is keenly felt, of cherishing moments of closeness, of
enjoyment, of contentment. And anniversaries are times of memory.

6.27 p.m.,
Tuesday, 22nd November 2005

My darling,
*I write to the strains of Gounod's 'Judex'. How apt! It is forever a
reminder of our last evening in Athlumney, Navan, before we
moved to Greystones. This is a day of memory (isn't every day?),
because on this afternoon forty years ago I entered 'the Blanch', and
thus changed forever your life and mine (if only you knew what was
coming, you would have done a 'flit' ...). Me? I'm just so thankful
that it was so and I thank you, thank you, thank you. The words of
Shakespeare come to mind:*

> There's a divinity that shapes our ends
> Rough-hew them how we will ...

It is an age ago and I was so gauche and green (I know, I know, she said). It took me three months to find you, but what a find. I MEAN THAT. I still don't know – and never will I suppose – what you saw in me, but THANK YOU. Anyway, I'm home from London where we celebrated the christening of our granddaughter, Georgia. We had a lovely week there. Wrote you some haiku – hope you like them.

13th–18th November 2005

THREE LONDON HAIKU

Champagne, fun, laughter
At Georgia's big party
You gliding, laughing

—

We walked Old Bond Street
Gucci, Tiffany's, Prada -
What damage you'd do!

—

A Hampstead Heath fact
Sixteen hundred and five days
Of me minus you …

And now I'm home to fog and frost. Yeuch! Read one of your letters where you said how you hated the fog at sea – claustrophobic!! Love those letters. Love their author. Did, do and will. But today is about 'the Blanch' – the new boy in Unit 2, having a boiled egg for tea and unknowingly entering the Great Adventure, little knowing that across the field on that murky grey November evening lay his dream …
At the risk of boring you, THANK YOU – forever.

Love, John x

Place is of course very much associated with memory. It was that memory of an autumn evening relaxation with Olive in St Stephen's Green that led me to dally there heartbroken a year later – and be rewarded with a meeting with her angel … Although we never went back as a couple to Loughnafooey – that magical place in Connemara where I proposed to Olive – I have gone back a number of times since her death, to recapture the memory, to recapture her presence.

Wednesday, 17th September 2008

LOUGHNAFOOEY '08

Silence
Save for the music
Of river and rivulet
And the happy chattering
Of birds
Welcoming a day
Stolen from summer.
Warm sunshine
On a dappled lake
A gentle breeze
(You are here!)

I cast a rose
From my garden
Into the singing river.
Amazingly
It fought the flow
And twice sought
The bank-side pool
Refusing to leave.
(You are here!)

The house derelict
The dog no more
The tree in bloom
Like the memory
Of a question
And a kiss

And the glorious response
Of a three-eyed woman

You are in your heaven
I am in mine
But all is well.
Like the rose
You refuse to leave

The place does not have to be wild and beautiful, like Loughnafooey, to evoke memory. Just beyond the laneway to Olive's family home in Stackallen is a gateway to another farm. Here, in our courting days, we would snatch a few golden moments on Sunday evenings before parting for the week ...

8.55 p.m.,
7th December 2006

ROUNDTREES' GATE

Thinking a lot
Of Roundtrees' Gate
For some reason ...
Stolen moments of delight
On fading summer evenings.
A touch, a kiss
– so tender –
And then again, a touch
And kiss.
Fingers clasped
And fondled.
A rabbit skips
Up the laneway.
No need to speak
Sheer happiness.
Thank you.

Some people express surprise that I return each year to Kelly's Hotel in Rosslare for the anniversary of Olive's death. Does it not 'bring it all back'? Yes, but it also brings back memories of contentment and happiness. Our children maintain they feel closer to their mother there than anywhere else. I always sense that a part of Olive's spirit never left Rosslare. I see her everywhere – relaxing on a sun-lounger, strolling on the beach, elegant in the dining-room. To maintain her presence there, I presented the hotel with a memorial sculpture by John Behan – a flight of birds that seem to capture her free spirit. So going back to Kelly's is a little bit of going home.

5.15 p.m.,
Friday, 26th March 2004

WELCOME

Sitting beside
Your sculpture
In the log-fire lit
Lounge of Kelly's Hotel
I reach across
And touch
Those Behan birds in flight
That capture your spirit
So …

The fire crackles, dances.
Warmth
Comfort
It is good to be here.
Little wonder that
Eddie Cullen's words of greeting
Were
'Welcome Home!'

And then there are the photographs – true testament to the living of ordinary lives. Shortly after Olive's death I assembled an album of photographs that had hitherto been scattered in boxes, drawers, books. It has grown over the years as more photographs have been unearthed in the most unlikely places. It is a treasure-house of memory for me, bringing 'roses in December', to use Brendan Kennelly's beautiful phrase. I bring it with me on my travels (I was actually leafing through it when I encountered the angel in St Stephen's Green) and the last thing I do each night is to kiss my way though random pages ...

Thurles,
5.25 p.m.,
29th November 2006

THE MOMENTS AND THE DAYS

Leafing through
My photo album
It occurs to me
There were so many
Moments of delight
In so many places
Over so many years.
So
Despite our differences
Our flare-ups
And deep freezes
There is so much
To be thankful for.
So
Thank you for the moments
Thank you for the days.

Holding on to memories is an important part of the grieving process but letting go is equally important – letting go of the physical reminders of the presence of the loved one.

Good friends Pat and Phelim Donlon
throw a 60th birthday party for me

With John O'Donohue in Ballinderreen

At Eva Perón's Tomb,
Recoleta Cemetery, Buenos Aires

Iguazu Falls, Argentina

In Red Square, Kremlin

Auschwitz

Birkenau   *At Zaccheus' Tree, Jericho*

In Chekov's Garden

Tolstoy's House

Christmas in Clarinbridge, 2007. Myself, Eva, Deirdre, Georgia, Declan, Lisa

Presenting a copy of Goodnight Ballivor, I'll Sleep in Trim *to President Mary McAleese*

With Seamus Heaney and Ken Whitaker
at the launch of The Curious Mind

Receiving an honourary doctorate, University of Limerick, 2003.
From left: Myself, Anna Manahan, Roger Downer (President of UL),
Bill Whelan, Tom Hyland, Bruno Giuranna

The John Behan Sculpture, presented to Kelly's Hotel
in memory of Olive (see p. 159)

Declan and Kelly's wedding, with John and Lisa Hendy, myself and Deirdre. At front, Georgia and Eva Hendy.

Olive, on the way to the Aran Islands, early 1960s (see p. 182)

Moving house in 2005 was very emotional. My last act on leaving Otterbrook was to visit each room and touch each light-switch that Olive would have touched … Disposing of her clothes was even more traumatic – clothes were so much her signature. Each jacket or dress had a memory. And then there were the handbags.

10.30 p.m.,
Tuesday, 24th February 2004

My darling,
Dee is here from the U.S. Tomorrow we start barrowing ten tons of gravel to make a patio – I eventually got around to it after thirteen years! Tonight over dinner we talked of you – not critically – just trying to analyse the enigma that was you. What was going on in your head over those last ten years? Happy here, yes, but unhappy in other ways. Disillusioned with life? With me? 'Wanting to be alone'? A conundrum – but aren't we all conundrums? Do we ever really know ourselves? Or each other?

Earlier Dee began going through your handbags – all sixteen of them! So I decided to finish the job I had started two years ago. And it was all there – A Life – in the clutter and flotsam and jetsam of many years. A bill from Slowey's for a hat (£14/11/6!) in August '68. Your pink 'going-away' hat? The endless cosmetics – free samples, nail varnish, Swedish Formula (how often I went in pursuit of them!). The hated inhalers. Tablets and pills, emery boards. The beautiful letters the children wrote to you when you were ill in 1983. A bill from Geoghegan's (19/11d) for a babygro in 1969. A photo of Fr Michael O'Neill and Michael O'Leary speaking at a Vietnam protest meeting in 1968. An invitation from me to The Open Mind Guest Lecture in 1999. A receipt for £1 for a Pathology Test in Drogheda in 1969. A postcard from your friend Carlos in Portugal ('I am regular. Not forget me!'). A Life – in all the shreds and patches and bits and pieces of everyday living. Chequebook stubs, bank statements, address books, a memoriam card of your grandfather.

A Life. A Life. And I loved you in each unorganised, messy particle. I bought a new car on Friday. Letting go of the old one was letting go of another part of you. And Dee is here. And tomorrow we spread gravel.

Enigma, mystery, conundrum – I love all of you.

John x

As Joxer puts it in *Juno and the Paycock* – 'For memory is the only friend/That grief can call its own.'

John O'Donohue was right. In the kingdom of memory, nothing is lost or forgotten. There are reminders of Olive at every turn – thankfully.

2.05 a.m., 25th March 2003
(21 months on)

FIFTEEN THINGS THAT REMIND ME OF YOU

Champagne, Tio Pepe
And Chablis too
Edith Piaf
And Ray Charles
Singing the Blues
A Jane Austen novel
A Tchaikovsky
Adagio
A jacket from
Paul Costelloe
(In cream, of course)
Frost and Poirot
And Inspector Morse
A 'Tup of Tea'
A little Note
And from Day One
A Black Leather Coat.
And Laughter –
Always
Always
Laughter.

Yet in this heart's most sacred place
Thou, thou alone, shalt dwell forever;
And still shall recollection trace;
In fancy's mirror, ever near,
Each smile, each tear, that form, that face, –
Though lost to sight, to memory dear.

(From 'Good Bye' by Thomas Moore)

Regret

Memory is of course a two-edged sword. There are memories of bad days which can equally be dredged up from the unconscious by a photograph, a piece of music, a worthless trinket. Memories of lost opportunities – 'moments that we had and did not treasure', as Ann Henning so aptly puts it. What was I (were we) at, that we couldn't savour those moments? Things said, when silence would have been the wiser option, when you could not resist the 'smart' comment, the cynical aside, the sarcastic jab. Hurt is caused and inevitably there follow counter-comments leading to a heated argument and ultimately what Olive described as the 'deep freeze', when no one talked for hours or days … Other couples refer to it as 'silent movies' or 'vision-no-sound'. It passes, of course, as all things do, but when the death of a partner comes, those moments come back to haunt us. 'If only' moments.

And then there are the things unsaid. Opportunities not taken to say words of comfort, understanding, praise. To say those three little words – 'I love you' – that you couldn't say often enough or passionately enough during courtship days. Seamus Heaney tells a poignant story of a man from his homeplace who had difficulty engaging with the opposite sex. When he finally managed to take out a woman, the curious neighbours enquired if he would be seeing her again. 'Do you know,' he replied, 'she never said …' All of our stories are littered with 'never saids'. When grumpy old Victor Meldrew dies in the final episode of *One Foot in the Grave*, his much put-upon wife, Margaret, observes, 'There are a lot of things you never say that you think about saying, but life goes on …'

Things said. Things unsaid. Things done. Things not done. As psychologist Marie Murray wrote in her *Irish Times* column, 'Mind Moves':

> It is the irretrievability of opportunity that deepens regret ... That is why regret is time-related. It is often expressed as a wish that one could turn back time, take a different, wiser path, follow a road less travelled, choose another route, alter a response, change a relationship, amend past incidents or even alter the entire course of one's personal life.

Further, Marie adds, 'regret allied to guilt is usually toxic'. What to do? I return to my Galway neighbour, quoted earlier: 'If you didn't travel the road you travelled, you wouldn't be where you are now ...' It's the path you took in life that makes you who you are now. Marie Murray agrees:

> After all, the road we did not travel might have been bumpier than the one we chose. We cannot tell. Maybe the richness of life would have bypassed us if we had taken more predictable paths. Maybe what we did and said, and what was said to us was enough – and if we wished that it was more or less, that may be because we have insight now rather than that errors were made at that time. For we need to remember that the unsaid is usually known, that when we regret what we did not do in the past, it is from the perspective of the present that we make that analysis. We probably did what we could at the time, and we should not judge ourselves by what would be possible for us to do today.

Betty, a widow after a forty-year marriage, wrote to me after the publication of *Sea of Love, Sea of Loss*:

> I am sorry for the time wasted, when it was 'all picture and no sound', but they were just the knots in the myriad of threads and colours that made up the priceless tapestry that was our life together. We're only human after all.

Of course we are – human in our strengths and in our weaknesses, in our constancy and in our fickleness. And if it was human to fail sometimes, it is equally human to regret those failings or to entertain doubts that linger long after the loved one has gone.

Friday, 19th October 2007

TWENTY MONTAUK QUESTIONS

1. Do you love me – as I love you?
2. Do you miss me – as I miss you?
3. Did you regret marrying me?
4. Did I disappoint you?
5. Did I bore you?
6. Did you tire of me?
7. If so, why ...?
8. If so, when ...?
9. Why do I have weird dreams, like last night's?
10. Am I annoying you now, asking these questions?
11. Do you realise how much you consume my every day?
12. And that I would have it no other way?
13. Do you know how much I regret lost opportunities?
14. Do you regret same?
15. Do you know how grateful I am to you?
16. Do you know how much I crave your forgiveness for any hurt or unhappiness I caused you?
17. Do you know how I need you, this and every day?
18. Do you know how nothing I am without you, despite all my 'successes', 'achievements' etc.?
19. Do you know that you are increasingly, each day, the most beautiful creature on this or any planet?
20. Do you know how totally, purely, indescribably and forever I love you?

(With a cigar and a Baileys, listening to Legends 990 FM (currently playing 'Promises, Promises'!!) on the last night of our visit to Montauk, Long Island, USA.)

This may all seem like an ongoing guilt-trip, which in part it is. Ridiculous to some, unnecessary to others, but personal to me. Again and again, I am grateful for Marie Murray's insights:

> Grief is relentless. It finds ways of admonishing, reminding and ruminating. It is seldom predictable. While universal in pattern, it is personal in its particularity … Guilt finds the moment of carelessness in a lifetime of devotion; the one request refused in the generosity of giving; the minute of anger in a marriage that was a loving relationship. This is why people often have regret at what now seems like neglect, if romance was ridiculed, a gift not given, love not romantically conveyed … Guilt forgets that one single day does not define a relationship; that love is not always articulated in conventional ways.

Those are comforting words. I am reminded of the words Anne McCabe had inscribed on the gravestone of her husband Jerry, murdered by the IRA in 1996: 'Married couples who love each other tell each other a thousand things without talking …'

For all that, guilt and its partner regret are relentless in insinuating themselves into a life, drawing on their old allies – doubt and fear. We are in the dark. We must be patient.

> If each day falls
> inside each night,
> there exists a well
> where clarity is imprisoned.
>
> We need to sit on the rim
> of the well of darkness
> and fish for fallen light
> with patience.
>
> (Pablo Neruda)

Guilt and regret may seem an indication of negativity but Marie Murray strikes a positive note to end on:

> Grief for another is the ultimate marker for that other. It anoints with remembrance. It embraces with regret. It enfolds the person who was loved with loving recollections.

> If life for me hath joy or light
> T'is all from thee;
> My thoughts by day, my dreams by night,
> Are but of thee, of only thee.

(From 'T'is All For Thee' by Thomas Moore)

Letters

Nobody suggested it as a therapy, but a month after Olive died I picked up my pen and wrote to her – after a gap of thirty-three years. To me it seemed the most natural and obvious thing to do. Letters had played such a huge role in our lives – from the day I wrote that first (cringing!) letter in German. To a large extent I had wooed and won this beautiful woman by letter. And yes, it has occurred to me that maybe I was more impressive on paper than in reality – but every letter was straight from the heart. Nine years on, as I read that letter of 26th July 2001, that heart sings and cries with the same emotion. I would not alter a word of it.

'But how can you continue writing to someone who is *gone*?' some people will ask. Simple. For me she is not gone. Physically yes, but in every other way, present. And I write to maintain that presence.

'But there is no correspondence,' they say. 'She can hardly write back.' No, but I can still converse with her. I know her (I think!). I know the interests we share. I know what would concern her, what would make her laugh.

10th July 2008

My darling,
I just HAVE to record this! I have just been watching a TV documentary about Grace Kelly's fairytale romance. As you know (didn't you?!) I was a strong contender there … She had class, elegance, poise, looks (but of course never reached your level – TRUE!). Anyway, when the narrator told of Grace's engagement to

Rainier in January 1956, I turned to you and told you how I had been totally DEV-AS-TATED, particularly as I had to sit the Intermediate Cert Exam that year. And when she sailed for Monaco in April, I had only two months to swot for the exam. No wonder I had to repeat it in 1957! I had a brief dalliance with the South African tennis player Sandra Reynolds that year (on the rebound!) but that didn't work out either. A loser in love twice by the age of sixteen – no wonder I went off the radar for ten years until you walked into my life (unfortunately, says she!). Am I mad or what? Don't answer that!

On a more positive note, I met Donal Haughey today. He is keen to make a TV documentary on Goodnight Ballivor [my 2008 memoir]. *And today also I listened to an audio-tape of Declan's third birthday party. It was so lovely to hear your voice, but so unreal – as if nothing had ever happened …*

I wonder did Grace ever regret dumping me.

Love, John x

Silly stuff, but meaningful to me. I just hope I gave Olive a giggle, but letters are equally important on the 'down' days when the loneliness creeps in like a fog.

Clarinbridge,
11th June 2005

My darling,
I'm sitting out on the patio of my new home in Clarinbridge on a glorious summer evening. The lawn is newly mown. My flowers are beginning to grow – at last. My potatoes and shallots are thriving. It is so peaceful. I have so much to be thankful for (and I AM) but I am desperately, desperately lonely for you. Unbelievably. I seem to miss you more in summer, because you were a summer person, I suppose. I just miss your presence, seeing you relax in the sun. Miss your scent, your languid walk, your small-talk, just seeing you around. The tears flow. Don't talk to me about 'time the healer'. Rubbish.

I know you would love this place. I also know I wouldn't want you to be anywhere else than where you are now – the ultimate home – but I just want you to know how much I miss you around the place. Despite all our problems, no-one but no-one can or will take your place. In a curious way, I am happy that I am so lonely! It's just a tribute to you, what you were, what you meant to me, and to the absolutely pure and bottomless love I have for you. All I ask is your love and your spiritual presence. Without them – without you – I am NOTHING.

I've been reading your mum's diary which you kept – and loving every little reference to you: walking at fourteen months, ill at two, crying to go to school with Joan, and most of all at age five, bringing in the first primroses of spring to your mum.

'I hope I will always remember Olive as she rushed to me with the primroses in her hand, her face alight, in her little blue frock and pink cardigan ...'

Totally exquisite!

Love you.
John x

There are moments you want to share and which you know you would enjoy sharing.

1.10 a.m.,
Sunday, 13th July 2003

My darling,
There's a terrifically bright full moon out there – and I love you so much. Beginning and end of story. Not the end, I hope! I'm really suffering this week – very down, very lonely. Little energy or enthusiasm. Why? Felt you might have 'wandered off' on me again. Wouldn't blame you. A friend came to the rescue with another letter, saying 'you wanted love and love is what she sent ever since she went. It is a mystery, but if we believe there is no beginning and no end, then we need to face the challenge that she is, always was, ever will be yours ...'

Isn't she uncanny? Isn't she your angel? Thank you, I HAVE to believe that. I desperately, desperately want to believe that. I know I'm being impatient and boring, but I believe, I believe, I believe. I really am down and very lonely this week. VERY LONELY. It gets worse with time, if anything. I'm doing my best. Writing bits. Walking. But ...

The one bright spot was OUR picnic on Thursday for L'Arche Group from Belfast who came with Maria Garvey. I had eleven adults here (we had, knowing your love for the disabled) and we had a great time. I joined them for dinner in Ballyvaughan later (I supplied my new potatoes!). They are such dotes – Geoffrey, who held my hand all through our walk; Thomas, the 'severely damaged one'; Gillian ('I am beautiful'); and Larry, beautiful Larry, the mystic who spends hours watching the clouds ... Beautiful people. More of your angels.

Please be with me now – always. I believe.

John x

A television series evokes memories. Share them!

9th December 2007

My darling,
I've just been watching Cranford *on the BBC – with you, of course. Sheer joy. It is so you. 'I fear my sister has had a nervous eclipse ...' 'Where blossoms lead, love will follow ...' (The seed in your heart...) I can hear you chuckling at Dr Harrison's dilemma – three women in love with him. We, of course, walked out together in* Cranford *style – even if I didn't ask your father's permission!*

It was a beautifully measured and natural courtship – our way, our pace, our time. I've been thinking a lot about those lovely days – the precious weekends, Sunday tea in Iveleary Road, and those tender moments at Roundtree's Gate ... Cranford *moments, surely. Enough to give you a nervous eclipse! I thank you, I thank you, I thank you. I savour those memories fiercely.*

And the final act each night … Leafing through the album is an untiring delight. You continue to consume my days. Thank you.
   Forever.

John x

And there are the anniversary days that must be commemorated with a letter.

1.20 a.m.,
Monday, 5th October 2009

My darling,
Just past the fortieth birthday of our firstborn, Lisa. I have to write and say – thank you for the sheer and indescribable joy I experienced on that wonderful day. I've been going through the letters I wrote then (thank you for keeping them).
   '… so proud, so privileged to have you as my wife and mother of our child … I knew I would be so, the very first day I saw you. So glad I did see you – think how unfulfilled my life would have been without you …'
   Even then, I wrote:
   'I was born on March 1st 1966 …' 'My waking thought to my sleeping prayer is you, you, you. Always, through eternity.' And now it has come to pass, forty years on. I reached such heights that day …
   'My wonderful, beautiful darling; my cherished and adored one, my everything. My life, my love, in whose love I find complete fulfilment, who makes me feel so contented and so full of love. Truly, my cup runneth over.'
   … Heights I never thought I could reach again – until NOW. Of course the intervening years brought rough and difficult times which continue to haunt and wrack me, but here and now I can honestly say I am back up there again – loving you, longing for you, feeling so proud and privileged, so grateful, so totally overwhelmed, so totally, absolutely, purely and unconditionally IN LOVE WITH YOU.

It is wonderful. It is beautiful beyond words. I am so blessed to be in love like this all over again. I may be lost and lonely, but I am so HAPPY! I don't think anyone but you could understand that I am so close to you, so so close. You consume every waking hour. You know that. You must know. All I need to know is that you feel the same.

As for Lisa, she got a deer's head mounted on the wall from John … (can't see you longing for that!). But she's happy. And she got a Gucci bag from me … (CAN see you longing for that!). All I know is that forty years on, life is even more beautiful. I love you so very much, Olive McKeever. As I wrote then …

'I don't know which I owe most to – you or God! Anyway, I adore you both!'

The seed in my heart blossoms riotously, wonderfully. Thank you my beautiful one.

John x

P.S. When I spoke to Lisa on the phone today, 'Clair de Lune' came on the radio. You again?

Letter-writing is, I suppose, passé now. A lost art in an era of texting and emails. Instant communication. A pity, since the discipline of the letter taught us to be reflective, to be personal, to be intimate. Letters reveal our personalities. When Olive (thankfully) replied to my letters all those years ago, her personality revealed itself in every line. Whether it was her caring nature or her impish sense of humour, her letters were (and remain) so sparky and so spontaneous. Equally, she loved my letters (More! More! More!) and what started as an innocent pursuit to relieve the boredom of institutional life gradually came to mean so much more. Forty years on, not a lot has changed – for me.

Midnight,
Christmas Day 2006

My darling,
Happy, happy Christmas. It's well for you'se up there (as Kay would say) – it's Christmas all the time for ye! Enjoy! Sitting here at the end of a long day, smoking a cigar, sipping a single malt Black Bush, listening to George Michael (memories of clearing out 'Sunset' before our big Into the West adventure …) The family are all here and happy, but we're missing you. They are watching Love Actually. *I've already seen it and I'm in love actually anyway … Must introduce you to HER. You'd love HER. It's for real and forever. I'm so happy and hope you're happy about it too. (Please tell me so!)*

Well, she is absolutely STUNNING, elegant, graceful, loving. I'm absolutely crazy about her. My love deepens every day and she grows more beautiful every day. This is IT – forever. Can't stop thinking about her. I thank the Lord for her every day. She's an absolute SAINT! She is everything to me. Everything. Of course – I forgot. You introduced her to me. Thank you. Looking forward to that eternal Christmas. I leave you to the haunting strains of 'Cowboys and Angels'. Not leaving you, EVER, actually. Go figure! Love you beyond telling.

John x

P.S. Your favourite ABBA song was on earlier – 'I Have a Dream' (and then along came J.Q., ses you!) Sorry, but it's LOVE ACTUALLY …

Most of all, the letter is a conversation about the minutiae of the day – news of the world, news of family, the concerns that cross your mind on any given day, however ephemeral, however strange. Long live the letter!

1.27 a.m., Tuesday, 24th February 2009
My darling,

I know it has been a month since I wrote but I've been BUSY … On Sunday night I finished the Book of Meath. *I can't quite believe I wrote it in seven weeks. I suspect your beautiful hand at work there. Thank you. I'm quite happy with it.* Now it's back to The Curious Mind … *Busy with talks (one to sixty retired nuns at Knock!) and school visits.*

The recession deepens. Declan is hanging on. This is not the time to be an auctioneer … Lisa is worried about world anarchy! She may have a point … The whole economy thing is so depressing. What those bankers and developers were up to … and we are the little insignificant people who must pay for this mess …

Meanwhile I gave the homily at Sunday Mass – about living your vocation and keeping a balance in your life (or 'keeping the bubble between the lines', to use the marvellous spirit-level analogy that our local street-sweeper, Michael Monaghan, gave me …) It went down well (was that you I heard coughing ominously down the back?).

And I recall a recent dream in which I asked, 'Did anyone ever tell you that you are incredibly beautiful? …' I'm sure they did. Well, I'm telling you now – belatedly. Again and again I realise I was so blessed and privileged. Again and again I try to rationalise the difficult Killeenaran years. And I can't. And they haunt me. And you haunt me – as you promised! Don't stop, please.

I hang on to every memory. In the intimacy and privacy of our special world, I am at peace. The bubble stays between the lines. For that I thank you. No one else matters or suffices. Only you. Cole Porter got it spot on:

> Night and day, you are the one
> Only you beneath the moon
> And under the sun.
> Day and night… Night and day

Love, John x

> Always the years between us. Always the hour.
> Always the love. Always.

(Virginia Woolf's last words to her husband at the end of that wonderful film, *The Hours*.)

Gratitude

'The best form of giving is thanksgiving. Your book is a grammar of gratitude for Olive.'

When Mary Redmond wrote to me thus after reading *Sea of Love, Sea of Loss*, her words pleased me greatly, not just for their poetic form but also for the fact that she had appraised one of the main objectives I had in writing the book – gratitude to Olive for her life and her love.

As Henri Nouwen has said, it is only in retrospect that we fully realise the power and the depth of love. In *The Prophet*, Kahlil Gibran makes the same observation:

> And ever has it been
> That Love knows not its own depth
> 'Til the hour of separation.

With that realisation comes a great surge of gratitude for love, a surge that is often unbidden and consequently all the more delightful.

11th February 2006

POWER SURGE

Sometimes
Without any warning
And for no apparent reason
– watching television
reading, mooching –

> I experience
> A powerful surge
> Of love for you.
> An unremitting
> Overwhelming
> And totally beautiful
> Heart attack
> Of love
> And gratitude.

It is a very special blessing to be loved – a blessing that with the passing years we can take for granted. It is only when we see its absence in the lives of others that we realise how grateful we should be.

> I saw a man who had never known
> A love that was all his own.
> I thought, as I thanked all the stars in the sky
> There but for you go I ...

> *(Brigadoon)*

Of course, special days and special places will always deepen the gratitude.

In the Garden,
Kelly's Resort Hotel, Rosslare
3.15 p.m.,
25th June 2008

My darling,
That day, that time, that place. Remembering. Remembering.
Remembering. We had Mass for you this morning. It still catches
the breath when the priest mentions your name. But it is so good to
be here (and I DON'T mean the food!) because you are here. I
wonder if you ever left ... I'm here in the 'Teahouse' just reflecting
on this afternoon seven years ago. How (Deo Gratias) we could just

be at ease by being here together. *Desultory conversation or none at all – but relaxed in each other's company, reclaiming lost time but, as it happened, too late ...*

How I love you now seven years on, with that total, pure, unconditional and unrelenting love – and I am so grateful. So it IS good to be here, close to you, walking with you, talking with you, carving your name in the sand, throwing a rose in the water – all the old things. It is so restful and it's because YOU are here ... The nightmare unreal memory will always be here too, but it is more than compensated for by your presence now – and by that photo album that I cherish so much and NEVER tire of 'reading'. So many smiles. Such elegance, radiance, unrivalled beauty. All I can say on this most sacred of days is all I ever say –

> *I LOVE you so much*
> *I THANK you so much*
> *I MISS you so much*
> *I NEED you so much.*

This day, this moment. Every day, every moment. I meet you everywhere. As Cole Porter put it –

> In the roaring traffic's boom,
> In the silence of my lonely room
> I think of you
> Day and night
> Night and day ...

Only you, ever you, always you. Please believe that, on this sacred, sacred day.

John x

It needs only a small thing to stir up the well of gratitude – '*Clair de Lune*' on the radio or a package arriving in the post ... In 2006 my brother-in-law Alan found some slides when going through his things. Eight photographs of Olive, taken in the early 1960s (before I came on the scene!). My photographer friend Ray Flynn developed them for me ...

13th July 2006

POSITIVE DEVELOPMENTS

They came in the post today
A mini-album
Courtesy of Ray Flynn
Eight stunning prints
Four from Southampton
Four from Inis Mór
Including one spectacular shot
Of you and cliff and sea.
I am
Totally overwhelmed
By your breathtaking beauty,
So proud
So in awe
So unworthy
They only deepen the mystery
Of how I won you.
Thank you
Multiplied by infinity.

A fortnight later came a special anniversary.

Thursday, 27th July 2006

My darling,
I don't have to ask if you remember this day thirty years ago!
Wonderful you produced a beautiful baby boy and made our life
and family and happiness complete. All I can say is all I ever say –
THANK YOU! You were wonderful, wonderful, wonderful and I
was so proud of you. Having traipsed around South Dublin house-

hunting through the boiling summer of 1976, you then produced Declan … Thank you, my love.

He has grown up to be a wonderful young man. I know you will look after him. He is doing so well – just got his exams (Thank you!). Otherwise, things are going well. The Sean Boylan book is nearing completion and I am 5,000 words into a new children's book (Thank you again!). As for those photos from Alan's slides, I feel so in awe, so unworthy. I know you will laugh, but I DO! Nothing compares to you. Do you understand? I am crying out for a sign, a message from your 'angels'. I know I'm odd and silly but I love you so much. It's harder and harder without you. It really is. But on this special day, thank you again for thirty years ago and for everything else in between.

Love, John x

Doubts persist. Did I disappoint Olive? Did I fail her in some way? I wish she would tell me! Yes, I must be patient but … In the meantime, the words of Patrick Kavanagh console me:

> So be reposed and praise, praise, praise
> The way it happened and the way it is.

(From 'Question to Life')

Detachment

I retired from RTÉ in December 2002 after twenty-seven years' enjoyable service with them. It was eighteen months after Olive's death but there was no causal relationship between the two events. If Olive were still alive, I would probably have retired then anyway. There are, however, parallels between the two events. Shortly before I retired, I produced a series on retirement – *Is There Life After Work?* There is equally a case to be made for a series entitled *Is There Life After Loss?* In both instances – retirement from work or the loss of a loved one – there may be the temptation to withdraw from living life freely and seeing only finality. Yielding to that temptation is literally a fatal move. Retirement is not an end. It is merely moving into a new phase of life. Similarly with loss. Writing to his father, Henri Nouwen said:

> Mother's death opened up for you a dimension of life in which the key word is not autonomy, but surrender ... Mother's death put your autonomy and independence into a new framework, the framework of life as a process of detachment ... Our autonomy is rooted in unknown soil. This constitutes the great challenge: to be so free that we can be obedient, to be so autonomous that we can be dependent, to be so in control that we can surrender ourselves. Here we touch the great paradox in life: to live in order to be able to die. That is what detachment is all about ... The death of a husband, wife, child or friend can cause people to stop living towards the unknown future and withdraw into the familiar past. They keep holding on to a

few precious memories and customs and see their lives as having come to a standstill … Mother's death is indeed an invitation to surrender ourselves more freely to the future, in the conviction that one of the most important parts of our lives may still be ahead of us and that mother's life and death were meant to make this possible.

Nouwen's notion of detachment, the freedom to progress to new, unexplored areas of life, I interpret as 'moving on', a clichéd phrase with which I am not very enamoured. In my own case it has been in large part realised by travels of both the physical world and the mind. In 2003 an old school friend of mine, Colman Morrissey, organised an opera tour to Russia and invited me to join his group. I am not an opera buff but it was too good an opportunity to pass up – to visit that mysterious land that darkened our childhoods with threats of world domination … We savoured the treasures and riches of the palaces and museums of St Petersburg before travelling on the overnight train to Moscow. The Bolshoi Ballet … the Kremlin … dreamtime! And of course I brought Olive with me.

Room 2613, Ukraine Hotel, Moscow
11.45 p.m.,
Thursday, 25th September 2003

My darling,
Have you just set me up? Just had a call from 'an old-fashioned girl, offering sex, massage …'

> *ME: No thanks.*
> *SHE: Maybe later?*
> *ME: No, not tonight! I have an early start in the morning. Goodbye.*

And this after a 7 a.m. wake-up call: 'The time of your arousal has arrived'!

I can hear you laughing. Earlier in the dining-room I heard the live band play 'Strangers in the Night' … Oh, you're haunting me alright! Thank you.

Today after a 200km bus journey we had two wonderful experiences.

First to Milkovo, to the home of Anton Chekov, where he wrote Uncle Vanya *and* The Seagull. *Absolute dote of a house and gardens, preserved as they were over one hundred years ago. You would love it. Such a sense of atmosphere – you almost expected to bump into the 'gentle subversive', as Colman called him. We had a brilliant guide to this wonderful place.*

Then on to Yasnaya Polyana, home of the Tolstoy family. Bigger house, huge estate. House not as intimate as Chekov's, but to be in his 'studies', the library, the vaulted room, dining-room, bedrooms – under the guidance of a lady who seemed to have walked out of one of his novels … pinch me! The beautiful wooded estate, the long silver-birch avenue, the autumn colours, the 'love-tree' and finally – in the heart of the woods – his plain, unmarked tomb. This was the experience of a lifetime.

I also found a beautiful second-hand book on Tolstoy and Yasnaya Polyana in the souvenir shop, to complete my day.

But I know you are still laughing at those phone calls …

Love, John x

Back home I was approached by O'Brien Press to write the text to accompany Colman Doyle's amazing archive of photographs spanning the second half of the twentieth century in a book entitled *All Changed* (2005). It was an opportunity to interweave my own journey through that period with the extraordinary events of those five decades that Colman had captured with his unerring lens. That association with O'Brien Press led subsequently to my co-writing *Sean Boylan: The Will to Win* (2006) – the autobiography of my great hero, a herbalist and former Meath Gaelic Football manager. This was the realisation of a long-pursued dream, prompted by a remark of one Olive

Quinn some years earlier. On hearing Sean give a public talk on being a manager, she said, 'There's a book in that fellow!' And of course, she was right. Thank you, my love.

In 2004 I went with Colman's Opera Group to Poland and Germany. The beautiful old quarters of Cracow and Wroclaw impressed, and we saw a spectacular production of *Madame Butterfly* in Berlin, but there could be only one deep, lasting impression from this tour.

Old Market Square, Wroclaw
12.30 p.m.,
Friday, 1st October 2004

My darling,
Greetings from Poland. Sitting in an open-air restaurant awaiting my lunch. What else is new? Come, join me.
What a couple of days! Wednesday – the unbelievable experience of Wieliczka Salt Mine, the largest in Europe. We only went down three levels out of nine, but it was amazing. Everything carved in salt, especially the huge St Kinga wedding church. Three hundred kilometres of labyrinths, lakes, even residential spas! A wonderful experience.
And then yesterday it was Auschwitz. There really are no words. You probably wouldn't have wanted to come. It was two hours of heartbreak. Through the brick quarters of Auschwitz One. The mountains of women's hair, of shoes, of suitcases with names painted on. The children's shoes. You don't want to be there, but you must. You don't want to know, but you do. You don't want to remember, but you can't escape. The punishment cells in Block 11, Fr Kolbe's cell, the standing-up cells. The execution courtyard between Blocks 10 and 11. The relentless murder of 1.1 million people. To stand in the gas chamber, to touch the incineration ovens … There are no words.
And then to Auschwitz Two – Birkenau. Although most of it is destroyed, the sheer vastness of it is terrifying. Almost as far as the eye can see. The wooden 'living' quarters. How they must have suffered, especially in winter. The railway tracks and the ramp for

decision – you live and work … you die. There are just no words but the place sears itself into your memory.

Being here has only made me cherish you all the more.

John x

AUSCHWITZ 30TH SEPTEMBER 2004

I do not want to be here
– but I am
I try not to remember
– but I must
I want to leave this place
– and I can
With my head full of
Cascades of hair
Mountains of suitcases
And shoes and shoes
And children's shoes.

They did not want to be here
– but they were
They tried not to remember
– but they did
They wanted to leave this place
– but they failed
Leaving only
Cascades of hair
Mountains of suitcases
And shoes and shoes
And children's shoes …

In 2004 Ireland held the presidency of the European Union, and to mark the occasion, Noel Dempsey TD, then Minister for Education, commissioned a book which would 'celebrate teaching and learning', to be given to visiting European ministers and dignitaries. I was flattered and honoured to be asked to write the text. To do this I drew on twenty-five years of radio work, distilling into print many of the interesting people and ideas I had encountered in that time. That text, enhanced by the brilliant photographs of Tom Lawlor, became *Ways of Knowing*. It was very well received but was never commercially published. My ambition was to expand it and publish it commercially. It took another five years to realise that dream, when Veritas published *The Curious Mind* in 2009.

In 2005, I joined up with a Galway group for a two-week visit to Argentina, another wonderful experience. There is only space here for fleeting impressions – the majestic broad streets of Buenos Aires; the magic of the tango; the incredible huge beefsteaks; the Recoleta – the city of the dead – mausoleums of the famous such as Eva Perón, Admiral Browne (father of the Argentine navy), boxing legend Luis Firpo, Fr Fahy from Galway – an extraordinary place, alive with cats! We spent St Patrick's Day in Buenos Aires where at a reception we met descendants of post-Famine emigrants who spoke with the flattest Westmeath accents ... Across country to Mendoza, city of plazas and wineries, north to the Brazilian border to the spectacular Iguazu Falls where an exhilarating powerboat trip took us *under* the falls – twice. East to Uruguay, by ferry to Colonia – the quaint sixteenth-century Portuguese town, partly caught in a time-warp with 1930s cars abandoned on the streets. And west to the Andes ...

Palm Sunday,
20th March 2005

My darling,
Today we travelled 200km from Mendoza on Route 7, reaching an eventual height of 3,200m. Absolutely breathtakingly spectacular drive into the Andes mountains – the colours, the formations, the height. The route followed that of the amazing Trans-Andean Railway, built by the Clark brothers early in the nineteenth century and in use until the 1970s. What an achievement! First stop was Uspallata (where Seven Years in Tibet *was filmed!) to encounter a Palm Sunday procession. Then we left Route 7 to see the fifteenth-*

century bridge built by Ambrosio O'Higgins (these Meath men get everywhere!). A very warm wind, known as Zonda (didn't he win the Irish Grand National?) – not good for the blood pressure! We went as far as the Las Cuevas international tunnel to Chile, but turned around as we had to be home in Mendoza for tea! Lunch in Puente del Inca, a walk through the sulphur baths and then up to the church of Our Lady of the Snows. Out of breath, but it was nice to get to a church on Palm Sunday. Deo Gratias to be here and to see in the distance the mighty Aconcagua mountain reaching into the clouds at just under 7,000m. A wonderful, wonderful experience. What a perfect day! Did you enjoy it? I felt very close to you on the way back – especially when Catherine from Connemara suddenly remarked, 'Wouldn't parts of this place remind you of Loughnafooey?' (where I proposed to you). Enough said, my love. Enough said! I love you so very much – in Loughnafooey, Aconcagua – wherever, whenever.

John x

Iguazu, 23rd March 2005

SOUTH AMERICAN SONG

I love you in Iguazu
Above the roaring falls
I love you in the Andes
Towering mountain halls

I love you in Buenos Aires'
Busy teeming streets
I love you in the forest's
Steamy sapping heat.

I love you in Mendoza
Its wineries and trees
In Lujan, Tigre, San Isidro
I cherish your company

> I love you in Argentina
> In Uruguay, Brazil
> I love you here, I love you there
> And always, always will.

Later that year, I went with Colman's group to Sicily. An added pleasure this time was the company of my daughter, Deirdre.

Hotel Baia,
Taormina, Sicily
Friday, 28th October 2005

My darling,
Here I am on the sixth-floor balcony alone with my thoughts – and you. Dee is below with the gang. They all love her to bits and she is really blossoming. We have been to Segesta, where our diva Pat McCarry sang for the group in the huge amphitheatre. Then on to Selinunte, another wonderful site of archaeological remains. I nearly forgot to tell you about a surreal evening in Count Federico's house in Palermo where we were entertained by Contessa Dorothy (another diva!) – with whom I 'fell in love' and duly got slagged by everyone! I was only acting the eejit (no problem to you, she said) and it was all a bit of fun. Tomorrow we're off to Mount Etna. Today? Today I bought an olive dish, just because it had the word OLIVE written on it. Once an eejit …

Con amore
Giovanni xx

10 p.m.,
Friday, 28th October 2005

TAORMINA AND YOU

I sit beneath
The Mediterranean stars
On the sixth-floor balcony
of Hotel Baia
Taormina.
In the inky distance
A ship disappears
Into the gloom.
Downstairs they dance
To 'That's *Amore*'.
Up here, peace.
I just sit and dream
Of Taormina and you.
That's *Amore*!

Also in 2005, I got back to writing for children with the publication of *Bill and Fred?* by O'Brien Press – the story of two eccentric older sisters who grew up in Africa and came to Ireland to inherit a house that is falling down about them … Busy times! In 2007 Fr Eamonn Dermody, parish priest of Clarinbridge, organised a pilgrimage to the Holy Land. A pilgrimage, not a holiday. A taxing schedule that would be a challenge, but again, too good an opportunity to miss.

There are no words to describe this experience adequately. I had never imagined it would happen and when it did happen, that it would be so meaningful and inspiring. To literally retrace the footsteps of Jesus, to have come to life all those places that were hitherto just strange names – Nazareth, Naim, Jericho, Caphernaum, Armageddon – sheer, sheer privilege. Again a few selected highlights …

Being a reader at Mass in Emmaus (mindful of Peter Hannon's parallel of the disciples on the road not recognising Jesus and my not recognising Olive in the Angel of St Stephen's Green ...) when the reading included the line 'The seed must die to blossom' ... In the Garden of Gethsemane, touching a 2,500-year-old *olive tree* that had witnessed Jesus' agony ... walking the Via Dolorosa through the twisting, smelly alleyways at 6 a.m., carrying the cross at the first and thirteenth stations ... Crawling under a Greek Orthodox altar to touch Golgotha (where Jesus died) through a hole in the ground and from there to the reputed tomb of Jesus ... Down the thirteen steps to the Nativity Grotto in Bethlehem – to Christ's birthplace marked by a star in the floor of a Greek Orthodox church ... Visiting Lazarus's tomb in Bethany ... crossing the Judean desert where Bedouins herd goats and sheep in a primitive lifestyle ... Bathing in the Dead Sea and sailing in a traditional fishing-boat on the Sea of Galilee ...

To Caphernaum, scene of many of Jesus' miracles, where he preached 'I am the Bread of Life' and called Peter, Andrew, James and John to follow him ... Being privileged to read the Beatitudes on the Mount of Beatitudes, with its breathtaking views of wheat fields, waving cypresses, banana groves – reminding you what an occasion the original event must have been ... Renewing baptismal vows in the river Jordan and marriage vows in Cana (when, out of the blue, Fr Dermody asked me to say something here, all I could think of was to tell the story of the Angel of St Stephen's Green) ... Mount Carmel, the Wailing Wall in Jerusalem, Mount Tabor ... the list goes on.

An inspiring, humbling and overwhelming twelve days' journey into the origins of Christianity, brought into the stark counterpoint of modern Israel by the location of our hotel in Bethlehem. At five o'clock each morning, Palestinians were queuing at the security gate to gain entry for work in Jerusalem. They queued along the grotesque thirty-foot concrete security wall that the Israelis have built around Palestinian territory. The wall across the road from our hotel abounded with graffiti such as 'They have the guns, but we have the numbers ...' and 'Why can't they see that what happened to them they are now doing to us ...?'

Another literary milestone came in 2008 when Veritas published my childhood memoir *Goodnight Ballivor, I'll Sleep in Trim* – a simple telling of life in a Midlands village in the 1940s and 1950s. I was very pleased with the reaction to it, especially from readers who wrote, 'I was never in Ballivor, but you wrote my story.' The local is the universal. I wrote that book primarily for my own children, two of whom – Deirdre and Declan – had accompanied me on a delightful tour of 'New England in the Fall' in 2007. We hired an SUV and drove at our own pace across seven states in ten days, savouring the delights of the trees of New Hampshire, of lovely towns like Woodstock in Vermont and Bar Harbour in Maine, of the golden beaches of Cape Cod and of the eccentricity of Provincetown – home to a large gathering of transvestites! The most important aspect of the trip, however, was the opportunity to share time and fun with my children – a 'bonding experience', as they like to call it.

12–17 October 2007

THREE NEW ENGLAND HAIKU

Pemigewasset
Kancamagus and Quechee –
Names tell history.

——

Seafood, stores and ships
Bar Harbour – once called Eden
Foolish change of name.

——

Provincetown image –
Parasol, flouncy dress, heels
And fishnets – HE'S PROUD!

In publishing terms 2009 was an extraordinary year, when, by sheer coincidence, I published three books in the space of three months, with three different publishers! After a long gap I linked up again with Poolbeg Press, who published *Specky Becky Bucks*, my sixth children's book – the story of Rebecca Jane Buckley, whose passion is Gaelic Football and whose dream is to play in Croke Park ... Next came Laurel Cottage Publications, who commissioned me to write the text for *Meath: A History and Guide to the Royal County*. I took great pleasure and satisfaction in recording the story of my native county. And finally came the realisation of a long-held dream when Veritas published *The Curious Mind* – an anthology drawn from twenty-five years of radio work. I was so honoured that my great hero, Dr Ken Whitaker, agreed to launch the book just days short of his ninety-third birthday. I am so blessed, but I suspect that the hand of Olive Quinn was at work there, as on many other occasions.

Galway Cathedral,
8.45 p.m., 17th July 2008

De ló is d'oíche	Day and night
Tusa, coíche	Always you
Am spreagadh	Urging me
Am mhealladh	Coaxing me
Tusa, coíche	Always you
De ló is d'oíche	Day and night

In that crowded year, 2009, I also found time to make a television documentary with Donal Haughey about my Ballivor childhood and to take a five-day trip to Vienna with Colman's opera group ... Is there life after work? Is there life after loss? Next question, please.

Milestones

In the ten years since Olive died, many milestones have been marked – retirement, births, weddings, moving house, distinctions achieved and publications. In every case it was important to maintain Olive's presence and to share those landmark days with her.

1.45 a.m.,
Christmas Eve 2002

My darling,
Lisa, John and our gorgeous grandchild Eva have arrived and we await Declan …
But to go back to an unforgettable night (Fri. 20th) in Studio One, the Radio Centre, RTÉ. My retirement party. I know I don't really have to tell you this – you were there, wrapping me in a blanket of security and love … What a turnout – Seamus and Marie Heaney, Garret FitzGerald, David Norris, John Lonergan, Sheamus Smith, my entire family and so many invitees and colleagues. Ronan Collins was MC (he had earlier played Ray Conniff – whom he HATES! – on his show for me). A totally wonderful occasion.
Speeches from Tim Lehane, Pat Donlon, Seamus Heaney, David Norris and many colleagues. Adrian Moynes, Director of Radio, presented me with the five-volume Field Day Anthology. *Ronan's 'Lucky Bag' contained a* Radio Fun Annual, *a Meath tracksuit (from Sean Boylan) and a brown envelope with a lot of money! … And then a procession of individual gifts – I filled ten bags! So much*

love. So much love. My speech went fine until I got to you – how I needed your hand for guidance, security, love ... I even told them of our engagement thirty-five years ago this week. It was all so unreal, so overwhelming. You should really have been there ... you were so much part of this traumatic, emotional day. Miss you like bloody hell. Said goodbye to my desk and chair and walked out of RTÉ at 10.45 p.m. after twenty-seven wonderful years ...

Earlier today Rosie Fitzherbert rang from Navan. Her mum remembers your giggles ... and every time she hears the Angelus she thinks of you. Isn't that the most lovely thing? I told her I always say the Angelus in memory of one who was ever faithful to it ... It moved me so much.

John x

In July 2002 a letter arrived on my desk from the University of Limerick, stating that at its meeting on 25th June (note the date – Olive's first anniversary) the Academic Council of the University had decided to award me an honorary PhD degree for my services to education and broadcasting. I was totally overwhelmed by this honour, which was largely brought about by the work of my good and longtime friend and colleague from our student-teacher days, George Cunningham. George wrote a wonderful citation for the conferring, which included these words:

> As all his programmes are ideas-centred works of art, crafted with precision, how apt are George Eliot's words: 'Art is the nearest thing to life, and its ultimate aim is to reshape the human consciousness, and with it the structure of society' ...

Conferring Day was 24th February 2003 – truly one of the most memorable and proud days of my life. My fellow-conferees were Anna Manahan, Tom Hyland, Bruno Giuranna and Bill Whelan.

Tuesday, 25th February 2003

My darling,
Well, here we are – home again. Myself and Deirdre (who is already asleep at 10 p.m.!), after the most incredible day of joy, celebration, pride – and longing. Impossible to describe. No need, I know, because you were there in the front row. It was wonderful, wonderful, wonderful. A lovely suite in the Castletroy Park Hotel (for us!). Monday was truly a day to remember – the Reception in Plassey House, the Robing, the Procession (the Pride!), seeing so many of our friends and families, the Citation, the Moment, the Applause, the post-conferring Reception. Kisses, autographs, hugs, congratulations, delight.

There are no words. There are no words. I know you don't need them. I wanted you there. You were there. I talked to you, loved you, saw your delight in it all. What a turnout! Family, neighbours, RTÉ colleagues, the Class of '61 from St Patrick's College (over twenty of them), friends, fans! It was the most wonderful day – as I said in my few words at the end of a beautiful dinner, second only to my wedding day. The only downside was that the woman who shared that day wasn't (physically) with me …

Back to the hotel. The party went on until 7 a.m. for some. My brother Noel on the piano, Sean Walsh reciting from The Merchant of Venice, *me singing 'On the Street Where You Live'. Mary Henehan toasting you with several bottles of champagne. My brother-in-law Dick Cotter belting out 'The Rose of Tralee' at 4 a.m. … There were a lot of sore heads this morning.*

It was your day as much as mine. And our three children charmed everyone. Well done – to you and me. WONDERFUL. Thank you for orchestrating it all. A last thought before I too collapse into sleep – Ann McGarry's words: 'If only we could realise eternity … Olive wouldn't want to come back.' I pray it is so. I want to realise it with you.

All my love,
Dr John xxx

The winter of 2003 brought another honour – and a very busy four months. I was invited to be a member of the judging panel for the IMPAC Book Award (with a prize of £100,000 for the winner). On 1st October, 125 novels were delivered to my doorstep, to be read and judged by February 2004 ... I spent the winter in pleasurable hibernation, but arriving at a shortlist with my four fellow-judges was hard work, and choosing an outright winner even harder.

Judging is such subjective work, with each of us bringing a different cultural and individual perspective to our choices. In the end, however, *This Blinding Absence of Light* by Tahar Ben Jelloun was a worthy winner, and the event was celebrated at a glittering occasion in City Hall, Dublin, in June 2004. Once in a lifetime is enough for such an intense process, in my opinion.

On 26th May that year Lisa gave birth to our second grandchild, Georgia, and it was another emotional moment when I first held 'Chubbychops' (as Lisa called her), appropriately in Rosslare, a month later. In that same summer I made the decision to move from Otterbrook – our home for the previous thirteen years. Moving is never an easy decision to make. A home has memories, presence, spirit wafting through its rooms, but I had to be pragmatic. Otterbrook was a unique house – two-storeyed, thatched, in a beautiful location (at the end of a boreen leading to the sea) – but it was now too big for me on my own and it was a house that needed regular maintenance. I considered going back to my native village of Ballivor in County Meath – for which I have a great attachment – but the past is another country. I would stay in the West. I was on my own and approaching my mid-sixties. I needed to be near services and shops. I had always liked Clarinbridge as a village. It is pretty and retains the village ambience, having kept the developers at bay. I found a comfortable, modern bungalow on the fringe of the village and took a gamble on purchasing it before I had sold Otterbrook. This proved a continuing nightmare for the next fourteen months as Otterbrook did not sell until July 2005, but I knew the Clarinbridge house was for me. I had a name for it straight away – *Sáimhín Só* (at my ease).

Sáimhín Só
Saturday, 16th October 2004

My darling,
Greetings from our new home! Hope you like it. I know it will never
be Otterbrook but this is me – on my own, with a chair, a saucepan,
a mug, a spoon, teabags and biscuits – just getting the feel of the
place since I collected the keys last week. And I like it. I really, really
do. Have been working out where everything will go and how things
work. I feel good here. I know it is for me – on my own. But you will
visit, won't you …?

Thursday, 21st July 2005

A CHAPTER ENDS

I have just left
Otterbrook
For the last time.
Not easy.
Said goodbye
To each room
Nook and cranny.
Touched each
Doorhandle, light-switch
You would have touched …
Silly, I know
But your spirit remains
In this now empty shell.
All I know is
You are happier now
Than ever you were here.
Come with me, love,
As I close the door
On a fourteen-year
Chapter
Forgive me for any

> Unhappy hours
> You spent here.
> Come, let us write
> A new and unending
> Chapter ...

In the summer of 2007 an unexpected and most lovely milestone popped up. As a teenager I had been an avid tennis fan. Not a player, just a fan. I would listen to Max Robertson's wonderful commentaries from Wimbledon on BBC Radio ... and when the tennis circus came to Dublin just after Wimbledon, I spent the week at the Fitzwilliam Club admiring my heroes and dreaming my dreams. I owned up to all of this in the award-winning 1992 radio documentary, *Ballyfin, a Boarding School Memory* (told in the third person, but my story) ...

> All the tennis greats came to Fitzwilliam then – Hoad, Drobny, Laver, Bueno – but they all paled in comparison with the lovely Sandra Reynolds, who was tall and slim and simply beautiful, her graceful movement like the gazelle of her native South Africa ... He scraped a half-crown together each day, just to be closer to Sandra Reynolds. She was – perfection. He had written to her once at Wimbledon, but no doubt she had a busy schedule. He understood. He loved Sandra Reynolds. Together they would be happy forever – even when they had retired after winning the Wimbledon Mixed Doubles for a record sixth successive time ...

Teenage dreams! Sandra wasn't just beautiful – she was a top-rank player. A beaten finalist in Wimbledon and in 1957 winner of both the Irish and South of Ireland Open Titles. Fifty years later, Ivan O'Riordan – a distinguished veteran of the Limerick tennis circle – thought it would be nice to invite Sandra back to Limerick to commemorate her victories. He tracked her down in South Africa and issued his invite. And she came! And he invited me also as a guest of honour ...

Friday, 29th June 2007

My darling,
Just back from Limerick, where last night we had the night of nights!
Fifty years on, face to face with Sandra Reynolds, whom I dreamed
and fantasised about as a shy, naive teenager, as she glided across the
courts at Fitzwilliam ... Was this another dream? I had to pinch
myself at times, but it was very, very real when I was called to speak
and pour my heart out as I had done in the Ballyfin radio
documentary. It was a magical night in Limerick Tennis Club –
thanks to Ivan O'Riordan, whose idea it was to bring Sandra back.

She really is a lovely person, and I was told last night that I had
caught her perfectly in the documentary and that she had not
changed a bit over the years. She is one genuine lady. It was such an
honour and a privilege to be part of a wonderful occasion (and it
will continue, with another banquet next Tuesday at Fitzwilliam!).
You would love her, but then you probably organised my being
there! Her husband Lowell was a pleasure to meet also.

Irony of ironies, the Tennis Club put me up in the Clarion Suites
Hotel – which used to be the Limerick Ryan, where we stayed on our
way back from our honeymoon in 1968 ... Sandra and I had a
'breakfast date' this morning before we parted – but I will see her
again next Tuesday in Fitzwilliam! I don't know. It's all so
wonderfully unreal, I am humbled and grateful. And I love you and
thank you for helping to make this happen. I am so blessed. So
many wonderful things have happened (like YOU!) and continue to
happen in my life. Not worthy! Thank the Lord and thank you.

Love, John x

So teenage dreams can come true – even if it takes fifty years.

Another major milestone was reached in 2008 when our son
Declan (affectionately known in childhood as 'Fozzie Bear')
married his long-time girlfriend Kelly Sheanon.

Farnham Radisson Hotel, Cavan,
25th May 2008

My darling,
Well here we are – recovering with a pint of Lucozade! – on the day
after the wonderful day before! Dec and Kelly's Big Day. What a
perfect day. Glorious sunshine. Glorious locations – the church in
Butlersbridge, the Derrygarra Inn and of course the Radisson Hotel.
You were SO there. It was an occasion made for you. You would
have outshone everyone and you would have been so proud of our
Fozzie Bear. He and Kelly were so happy – indeed there was so
much happiness all around. The Big Day was a total success – not a
hitch and a great mix of guests. Lovely church. Beautiful string
quartet. Of course it brought me back forty years to our own Big
Day, but you were here – proof of which was your niece Patricia
bringing me a photo of a young you on a stony beach somewhere. I
had it on the table all through the meal and mentioned it in my
speech, which went down very well, especially when I read the poem
'Trivia'.
I dreaded the dancing and had to take Ann Sheanon out on the
floor, but from there on I boogied away until 2 a.m. It was lovely to
see Lisa (in her Vivienne Westwood outfit) and Dee (in her little red
number) so happy on the dance floor. And of course Eva and
Georgia stole everyone's hearts as flower-girls. The abiding memory
is of the great surge of love and goodwill for the happy couple.
Thank you for Fozzie. He has come such a long way – very
successful in his career and now so happily married to the love of his
life. I hope he feels as I felt forty years ago. Please, please love me.
There is no-one else for me – despite your brother Peter teasing me
yesterday that it's about time I found a new woman! Not interested!
What we have we hold! Tomorrow, Dec and Kelly set off on
honeymoon to St Lucia. A long way from Glengarriff, ses you!
Sorry! It was the best I could do.
All the foregoing is overshadowed by the unexpected death of
your dear sister Joan on May 13th. She slipped away quietly, after a
short illness – a huge shock to us all. I hope you organised a big
'welcome home' for her. She would so have enjoyed our Big Day

yesterday. Thank you for all you put into it. And – try to remember!
– be mine.

Love you forever,
John x

On June 25th 2011, I arrive at another milestone – the tenth anniversary of Olive's death. For her, it is not even a blip in time, because there is no time in eternity. But for me it marks ten years of separation, loss, loneliness … all those things – but also a decade of blessings, growth and an ever-blossoming seed of love. I will mark this point in the journey quietly, with intense gratitude and with ever-mounting anticipation.

Love

Amo. I love.

Love. Probably no other subject has engaged the minds of songwriters, poets, novelists, artists and composers more than this little four-letter word. But what IS love? This question has haunted me ever since Olive's death ...

New Year's Eve, 2002

My darling,
Sitting here watching Gone With the Wind *on television. In ways we were like Rhett and Scarlett ... arguing, headstrong – but deeply in love! And frankly my dear, I DO give a damn! A million, million damns ...*

Monday, 8th December 2003

My darling,
Just felt the need to talk to you after reading the novel Lucca *(No. 40 on the IMPAC longlist!). The theme is – what is love? Now there's a question! I reflect on what we had ... So beautiful and perfect at the start. Then all the tangled, knotted threads. I would love to try to untangle them with you now, but I can't. Confused, frustrated. When I read these fictional lives, I wonder did we 'live' at all! Of course we did, but ... YOU lived, were loved by many. Me? Loved by you was enough then, is enough now. But the middle bit? Do you*

understand? Why couldn't we communicate better at times? Untangle the threads. Each time we tried, we seemed to tie more knots. Was that inevitable? I can see more clearly now. You can see it all now. So desperate to clear the confusion, Where do I turn? Doesn't change the way I feel for you. If only I knew how you feel. If only we could talk ...

I cherish utterly the way we met and fell in love. Utterly. Could have done better latterly – or was that how it was meant to be? And is that right? Wish we could talk. I'm probably being stupid but our story consumes me more and more, the more of these novels I read. By the time I get to No. 125, God knows what state I'll be in! What is love? What is love? And do you 'love' me now? Talk to me – please!

Wednesday, 10th December 2003

My darling,
'What is love?' was answered a couple of days later when I read through Volume One of these letters and a few from 1966–67. Pure, complete, beautiful love. Certain love. No doubts. No doubts – despite the middle bit. Why do I ever doubt? Listened to Mitch Albom (author of Tuesdays with Morrie) *talk about his new book* – Five People You Meet in Heaven. *Husband meets dead wife. She reassures him that love doesn't end. Memory is the key ... I second the motion!*

I'm currently reading an 800-page blockbuster set against a background of prostitution in Victorian London. It's all there, I tell you!

Love you so much.
John x

In *A Grief Observed*, C. S. Lewis grappled with the same 'death does not divide' dilemma:

If, as I can't help suspecting, the dead also feel the pains of separation (and this may be one of their purgatorial sufferings), then for both lovers, for all pairs of lovers without exception, bereavement is a universal and integral part of our experience of love. It follows marriage as normally as marriage follows courtship or as autumn follows summer. It is not a truncation of the dance but one of its phases ...

Let the dance continue! So what IS love? I can only offer a number of observations – not in any order of preference and most certainly not in the presumption that I excelled in any of them!

1. At its most basic level, love is simply willing the other well-being and happiness, thus establishing our own humanness. We need others to be human ourselves.
2. Love is enriching and fulfilling for the human spirit. I am a different person to the one that happened upon a 'vision in a black leather coat' in a TB sanatorium in 1966 – and a better person. Oscar Wilde expressed this in five simple words: 'Who, if loved, is poor?'
3. Love is patient. Love is kind. It is not envious, boastful or arrogant or rude ... (1 Corinthians 13:4).
4. Love is not always easy. To mix a couple of sporting metaphors, the 'state of the going' may change and sometimes 'the goalposts may be moved' at short notice. Love therefore demands adaptability and flexibility. When John O'Donohue writes of 'The Chalice of Your Love' ('For Love in a Time of Conflict'), he may well have meant the chalice to be interpreted as both the cup of giving and the cup of suffering.
5. Love represents a beautiful intimacy and closeness, but as Khalil Gibran reminds us in *The Prophet*: 'Let there be spaces in your togetherness.'
6. There are many ways of expressing love. It may require us to speak, or not to speak, to act or not to act. Love may indeed be 'a many splendoured thing', but equally it is a fragile thing

which, if not handled carefully, can be easily chipped or fractured. There is also what U. A. Fanthorpe called …

> a kind of love called maintenance
> Which stores the WD40 and knows
> When to use it;
> Which checks the insurance and
> doesn't forget the milkman,
> Which remembers to plant bulbs …

It's a long way from swooning under the moon in June, and may be seen as downright boring by some, but it is still valid and deserves acknowledgement in its own right.

7. Love IS lovelier the second time around – with the same person, of course …

8. In the end of all, love is pure mystery. Like the rose (often a symbolic expression of love) in the medieval poem by Angelus Silesius, it is *ohne warum* – without why.

> The rose is without why
> She blooms because she blooms …

Amo. I love. Amen. There abide faith, hope and love – these three. And the greatest of these is love.

Faith

Credo. I believe. So easy to say. So much more difficult to do. So much harder to explain.

I remember as a child sobbing my way through the Apostles' Creed, in anticipation of having it examined in school the following day. It was in a way a metaphor for how we learned then – through fear. Even though everything appeared 'through a glass darkly', we grew up in a tradition of faith and were steeped in a faith culture. There was the example of parents and community all about us. And there was the example of history. It may be considered passé now to speak of the ...

> Faith of our fathers, living still
> in spite of dungeon, fire and sword ...
> *(Frederick W. Faber)*

but it is nonetheless true that so many of our forebears were persecuted and died in defence of their faith. This is no small thing. If people were prepared to give their lives for their faith, then surely it is the 'pearl of great price' to be sought, cherished and nurtured above all costs.

Seven decades on, the light of faith still burns brightly for me. It is a simple faith born out of tradition, culture, example and, of course, education. There are many aspects of it that I cannot explain. It is mystery, but it is not a blind faith. I am assailed by doubt and uncertainty. I have stood on Skellig Rock and marvelled at the prayerful lives of monks who endured privation and penury there for over five centuries. I have stood in the gas chambers of Auschwitz and shuddered at the memory of the atrocities that were perpetrated there. How does one reconcile those experiences?

And all around me are wonder and incredible beauty. A starlit night. The amazing natural world as portrayed in the BBC television series *Life*. The poignancy of a Friel drama. The delicacy of a Heaney sonnet. The uplift of Mahler's *Resurrection Symphony*. There must be an Original Source. There must be – as Shakespeare says in *Hamlet*:

> A divinity that shapes our ends,
> rough-hew them how we will …

There must needs be uncertainty also. I am reminded of a wonderful talk on *The Power of Uncertainty*, which I recorded many years ago. It was delivered at a World Congress on Reading by Walter McGinitie. For him, uncertainty had great power within it:

> We may link uncertainty with fear, but it is the foundation of hope. We may link certainty with security, but it is the womb of indifference. Only a person who is willing to be uncertain can learn …

We may still see through the glass darkly, but within us lies the great creative force of the imagination – 'and its friend, possibility', as John O'Donohue puts it.

We are on a great journey of possibility which surely cannot end with death. I believe in an afterlife. A banner in our local church proclaims that 'in eternity everything is just beginning'. I like that concept – but what is the 'everything'? I do not know. I cannot know.

> Eye hath not seen nor ear heard, not hath it entered into the heart of man what things God hath prepared for those who love him. (1 Corinthians 2:9)

As St Paul said: 'I have not yet won, but I am still running …
racing for the finish to which God calls us.' It is mystery. It is gift.
It is a feeling of knowing that encourages me to struggle through
all the doubts and fears and uncertainties.

    Credo. I believe. There abide faith, hope and love – these three.
And the most emboldening of these is faith.

Hope

Spero. I hope.

The road of bereavement and loss is strewn with many consolations – most of which I have adverted to in this book.

Memory of and gratitude to the loved one, people – whether they be angels or complete strangers – who write, often to share their own experiences. Una Ryan sent me a copy of Rilke's beautiful poem, 'Death of the Beloved'.

> He knew only of death what all men may
> that those it takes it thrusts into dumb night.
> When she herself, though – no, not snatched away
> but tenderly unloosened from his sight –
>
> had glided over to the unknown shades
> and when he felt that he had now resigned
> the moonlight of her laughter to their glades
> and all her ways of being kind;
>
> then all at once he came to understand
> the dead through her, and joined them in their walk,
> kin to them all; he let others talk
>
> and paid no heed to them, and called that land
> the fortunately-placed, the ever-sweet –
> and groped out all its pathways for her feet.

In January 2008, in common with many people worldwide, I was deeply saddened by the untimely death of John O'Donohue. I recorded this in a letter to Olive:

It is just so hard to take it in. A man who was so full of life, dead at fifty-two. He was so good to me – in person and in his writing – when you left us. I went to the huge funeral in Fanore last Saturday. Drenched and frozen, but it was good to be there. His last book Benedictus *(a book of blessings) is such a treasure. 'For Love in a Time of Conflict' resonates so much with me.*

> When even the silence has become raw and torn
> May you hear again an echo of your first music.
> …
> Reach out with both hands
> To take the chalice of your love
> And carry it carefully through this echoless waste
> Until this winter pilgrimage leads you
> Towards the gateway to spring.

All I can say is yes and yes and yes and yes and yes.

Love, John x

P.S. I wrote these words in memory of John …

SOMETIMES

Sometimes
A voice is sent
To calm our deepest fears.

Sometimes
A hearty laugh
Will banish all our tears

Sometimes
Words will wing
Our dreaming ever higher

And sometimes
A mind will set
Imagination afire.

No man understood the human soul better than John O'Donohue.
His blessing 'For Grief' captures the journey of loss so well and
ends on an uplifting note:

Gradually you will learn acquaintance
With the invisible form of your departed
And when the work of grief is done,
The wound of loss will heal
And you will have learned
To wean your eyes
From that gap in the air
And be able to enter the hearth
In your soul where your loved one
Has awaited your return
All the time.

What he is pointing to here is the greatest consolation of all –
hope. Hope in the gateway to spring, to new life, to eternal life
and ultimate reunion with loved ones. Hope comes from trust in
the Lord who is 'the way, the truth and the life'. I was so honoured
to receive a letter of condolence on Olive's death from the great
bandleader Ray Conniff (who was the subject of a radio
documentary of mine). Ray's advice to 'help fill the void' was:

In all thy ways acknowledge Him
And He will direct thy path.

Henri Nouwen's *Letter of Consolation* to his father was written at
Easter time. On Good Friday he wrote:

If the God who revealed life to us, and whose only desire is to bring us to life, loved us so much that he wanted to experience with us the total absurdity of death, then – yes, then there must be hope; then there must be something more than death; then there must be a promise that is not fulfilled in our short existence in this world; then leaving behind the ones you love, the flowers and the trees, the mountains and the oceans, the beauty of art and music, and all the exuberant gifts of life, cannot be just the destruction and cruel end of all things; then indeed we have to wait for the third day.

On Holy Saturday, he wrote:

A silent, in-between time … a simple, quiet waiting with the deep inner knowledge that all will be well. How? Do not ask. Why? Do not worry. Where? You will know. When? Just wait. Just wait quietly, peacefully, joyfully … all will be well.

Writing the above passage into my *Book of Consolations,* I could only add 'Amen'! It found echo with another entry – from John McGahern's *Memoir*:

The best of life is lived quietly where nothing happens but our calm journey through the day, where change is imperceptible and the precious life is everything.

Finally, on Easter Sunday, Henri Nouwen writes of the Resurrection:

Doesn't this put mother's death in a completely new perspective? It does not make her death less painful or our own grief less heavy … but it makes us see and feel that death is part of a much greater and much deeper event, the fullness of which we cannot comprehend … What seemed to be the end proved to be a beginning … Suddenly a wall becomes a gate … Love is stronger than death.

In another letter of condolence, Joan Wilson expressed the same sentiment:

> Easter Sunday is always my best day. I go to the graves [of Gordon, Peter and Marie] early and recall the words that the angel said to the women at the grave – 'He is not here. He is risen.' Great words – they give me healing and the glorious hope that one day we shall all be united again in the presence of the Lord. All shall be changed. All perfect.

And from a friend who sent me these lines at Christmas 2002:

> And this will be heaven
> That will be heaven at last
> The first unclouded seeing
> To stand like the sunflower
> Turned fullface to the sun,
> Drenched with light
> The still centre held
> While circling planets sing
> With utter joy.
> Seeing and knowing at last
> In every particle
> Seen and known
> And not turning away again
> Never turning away again.
> (*Evangeline Paterson*)

In the words of Edith Sitwell:

> … Love is not changed by Death
> And nothing is lost and all in the end is harvest.

I wait, impatiently but quietly, for the harvest – in the knowledge that all will be well. *Dum spiro, spero.* While I breathe, I hope.

There abide faith, hope and love – these three. And the sweetest of these is hope …

2001–2011

A glorious decade for you
A sorrowful one for me
But a joyful decade too
When I think of what will be

Acknowledgements

MY THANKS TO

Pat Hunt, who started the whole thing off by asking me to 'write a piece on love and loss' for the Christmas 2001 newsletter of the Holy Redeemer Parish, Bray, Co. Wicklow, and also for his subsequent moving obituary in *The Irish Times*.

The Irish Times for permission to reproduce Olive's obituary.

Aidan Mathews for permission to reproduce his beautiful poem 'Watercolour for a Widower'. A line from that poem gave us the title for *Sea of Love, Sea of Loss*.

Ann Henning Jocelyn for permission to reproduce an extract from her collection, *Keylines*.

Michael Campion, sound operator at RTÉ Radio, whose skill and sensitivity were so important in the making of the radio programme *A Letter to Olive*.

The hundreds of listeners who wrote in response to that programme, many of them (notably Maeve Binchy) pleading with me to publish the story in book form.

Anne O'Neill, who typed the manuscript and encouraged me to write it in the first place, and to Máire Ní Fhrighil who typed the original manuscript of the sequel.

Treasa Coady of TownHouse who saw the possibility of a book in *Sea of Love, Sea of Loss* and who with Marie Heaney and Claire Rourke helped me realise the possibility with their guidance and suggestions.

Donna Doherty of Veritas who undertook the reprint of the original *Sea of Love, Sea of Loss* and who encouraged me to write the sequel, *Seed of Love, Seed of Life*, Caitríona Clarke of Veritas for her dedicated editorial work on this new edition of *Letters to Olive*, and Marie Murray for her thoughtful introduction.

John Quinn
February 2011

The author and publishers would like to acknowledge the following copyright material:

'The Whitsun Weddings' by Philip Larkin from *Collected Poems* (London: Faber and Faber 2003).

My Love When You Die' by Ann Henning Jocelyn, from *Keylines*, www.annhenningjocelyn.com.

'For Love in a Time of Conflict' from *Benedictus: A Book of Blessings* by John O'Donohue, published by Bantam Press. Reprinted by permission of The Random House Group Ltd.

'I Have A Dream' used by permission of Bocu Music Ltd. Composers B. Andersson/B. Ulvaeus.

'Appreciation – Olive Quinn' by Pat Hunt appears courtesy of *The Irish Times*.

'The Wishing Tree' by Seamus Heaney from *The Haw Lantern* (London: Faber and Faber 2006).

'All I Ask of You' from *The Phantom of the Opera*, lyrics by Charles Hart, additional lyrics by Richard Stilgoe, music by Andrew Lloyd Webber © copyright 1986 The Really Useful Group Ltd. All Rights Reserved. International copyright secured.

'A Cup of Sun' by Joan Walsh Anglund from *A Cup of Sun – A Book of Poems* (London: Collins 1968).

'Try To Remember' words by Tom Jones, music by Harvey Schmidt © 1960 (renewed) Chappell & Co., Inc. (ASCAP).